Praise for *Enslaved to Saved*

"Compliments to W. Reid Litchfield for his correct interpretation and insightful presentation of many New Testament metaphors. Twenty centuries have passed since the New Testament was written, and we do not easily relate to past cultures and circumstances. Litchfield explains the correct translation and metaphorical use in the New Testament of the words *slave* instead of *servant*. The subject is freedom of the spirit and mind, not freedom from physical slavery. The Christian seeking the higher road in his or her relationship to Jesus Christ will learn many useful insights and scriptural clarifications from this. In the process of reading this book, I have expanded my own understanding of drawing closer to Christ."

—William Victor Blacoe, author of *From Saul to Paul: the Road to Apostleship* and *Understanding the New Testament: 1st and 2nd Timothy, Titus, and Philemon*

ENSLAVED TO SAVED

Enslaved to Saved

The Metaphor of Christ as Our Master

W. Reid Litchfield

CFI
An Imprint of Cedar Fort, Inc.
Springville, Utah

ISBN 13: 978-1-4621-1604-1

Published by CFI, an imprint of Cedar Fort, Inc.
2373 W. 700 S., Springville, UT 84663
Distributed by Cedar Fort, Inc., www.cedarfort.com

LIBRARY OF CONGRESS CATALOGING-IN-PUBLICATION DATA

Litchfield, W. Reid, author.
Enslaved to saved / W. Reid Litchfield.
pages cm
Includes bibliographical references and index.
ISBN 978-1-4621-1604-1 (alk. paper)
1. Salvation--Christianity. 2. Slavery and the church--History. I. Title.

BT752.L58 2015
234--dc23

2015004548

Cover design by Shawnda T. Craig
Cover design © 2015 Lyle Mortimer
Edited and typeset by Kevin Haws

Printed in the United States of America

10 9 8 7 6 5 4 3 2 1

Printed on acid-free paper

Dedication

To Tiffany and our children: Tate, Ty, and Robyn.

CONTENTS

Chapter 1: Servant versus Slave in the New Testament

The Church of Jesus Christ of Latter-day Saints is a church of service. This tradition dates back to the earliest days of the Church's existence in the modern era. There are innumerable examples in which ordinary members have performed extraordinary feats of selfless service to others and considered it part of their duty to God. Today, the Church's theology, practice, and day-to-day operations are embodied by the belief that devotion to God and conversion to the gospel is manifest through service. To be a faithful believer is to be dedicated to the service of God—to be His servant.

There can be no doubt about the centrality of serving God as a pillar of Latter-day Saint doctrine if you consider just how frequently modern Church leaders have emphasized the principle of service. The doctrinal basis of this contention is also evident throughout the standard works. With this book, I will focus on the teachings of the New Testament to increase our worth and devotion as servants of God.

The earliest pages of the New Testament are rich with allegories about servants and doctrinal lessons about our role as God's servants after conversion. For example, hearing that she was to be the mother of the Son of God, Mary humbly replied, "Behold the handmaid of the Lord; be it unto me according to thy word."[1] She reiterated the idea of being a servant of God to her cousin Elisabeth in the beautiful passage known as the *Magnificat*.[2] Simeon, after seeing the infant Jesus, testified that He was the promised Messiah and said, "Now lettest thou thy servant depart in peace, according to thy word."[3] The followers of John the Baptist were called his servants.[4] Similarly, Jesus frequently referred to His disciples as His servants[5] and used the theme of servants in many of His teachings and parables. In fact, Jesus Himself came in the role of a servant.[6] He repeatedly emphasized the importance of the principle of service to others by teaching His disciples that the chief among them would be a servant of all.[7] Finally, after the death and Resurrection of Jesus Christ, His apostles and early Saints repeatedly referred to themselves as servants of Jesus Christ, servants of God, or as servants of the Church.[8]

And yet the tendency to view these passages from a contemporary viewpoint can be misleading. We must not forget that the books of the New Testament were not written in English, but in Greek.[9] And special effort is required to understand the context of these writings since they occurred almost two thousand years ago. Though relevant to today, the writings and teachings of God's servants in first-century eastern Mediterranean cannot be applied to contemporary times without carefully considering the context of when and where they were written. These facts are precisely why we face unique challenges in understanding the meanings of scriptures found in the Bible and why the process needs to be a lifelong endeavor. Parenthetically, this underscores the value of scriptures that were given to us in English in their primary form and in the modern era.

The notion of context is critically important in a study of what the New Testament teaches us about being a servant. For most of us, it's surprising to realize that the nine Greek words rendered as servant in the New Testament are more correctly understood if translated as "slave" in the vast majority of instances. Our current paradigm would hardly let us imagine the Savior teaching parables about slavery, or members of the Church attending meetings with their slaves—whom they viewed as their personal property. It would be equally difficult to envision members of the congregation so completely disenfranchised that they had no control over any elements of their day-to-day lives and could be bought or sold at the whim of their masters. Yet this was the reality of the times when our New Testament writings came into existence.

In his scholarly work entitled *Slavery and Society at Rome*, Keith Bradley made note of this tendency in the Bible. As an example, he cited the translation of 2 Timothy 2:24, in which masters and slaves are admonished to get along with one another:

> English translations tend to prefer "servants" and "Lord" for "slaves" and "Master" in texts such as these, diluting as a result the forcefulness of the original languages (or languages). But to contemporaries there could have been no doubt about the significance of the metaphor. The absolute authority of the object of worship over the worshipper was precisely the same as that commanded by the earthly slave owner over the slave, while the powerless subjection of the worshipper before God was exactly the same as that characterizing the earthly slave's relationship to his owner.[10]

Further analysis of words translated as "servant" in the King James Version (KJV) of the New Testament demonstrates this to be rather remarkably widespread. For example, in the eighty-one verses of the New Testament in which *servant* is found, the original Greek word is *doulos* or *douloo* in sixty-five. *Doulos* is the Greek word for slave or bondman and *douloo* means "to make a slave of." Virtually every other word translated as "servant" has some connotation of slavery, servitude, or bondage (see table at the end of this chapter). Similarly, many of the words we have traditionally associated with the humble servant of God have their origins in words that convey much harsher realities of bondage, slavery, or servitude. Such connotations—lost to us—would have been obvious to those living in the midst of a society that was dominated by slavery.

The observation that, in most instances, our New Testament should read *slave* whenever we encounter *servant* is hardly new and has been emphasized by a number of authors.[11] The lessons imparted by this understanding can be monumental. Nevertheless, this is a theme that is relatively undeveloped in Latter-day Saint literature. The degree to which this understanding changes New Testament messages can vary, depending on the passage, the reader, and his or her particular needs at the time. Certainly in some instances the message is the same, but in others the passages take on a new perspective. The promptings of the Holy Spirit given to the reader at the time of reading cannot be emphasized enough.[12]

Consider the parable of the prodigal son, in which Luke described the many years of service of the faithful son. In this case, the word *douleuo* is translated as "serve" in the KJV. The word *douleuo* can be translated as "to submit or give obedient service." However, *douleuo* can also be rendered "to be a slave."

After returning from his labors late in the evening, the faithful son was angry to find that his wayward brother had been received with joy and honored with a feast, while his steadfast faithfulness seemed to go unnoticed.

Luke 15:29–30

And he answering said to his father, Lo, these many years do I serve [*douleuo*] thee, neither transgressed I at any time thy commandment: and yet thou never gavest me a kid, that I might make merry with my friends: but as soon as this thy son was come, which hath devoured thy living with harlots, thou hast killed for him the fatted calf.

The faithful son's anger is palpable: *These many years I have slaved for you and never transgressed your commandments . . . yet I have been given nothing*. Though not a slave in any sense of the word, the faithful son nonetheless felt like a slave who had nothing while his prodigal brother feasted after his self-indulgent downfall to rock-bottom. We trust that this wise father was able to see through his faithful son's frustration and anger and teach him the big picture message of the incident.

Similar insights may be gained by reexamining Luke's account of Simeon's encounter of the newborn Christ. Consider the original Greek words translated as "Lord" and "servant" in this passage.

Luke 2:25–29

And, behold, there was a man in Jerusalem, whose name was Simeon; and the same man was just and devout, waiting for the consolation of Israel: and the Holy Ghost was upon him.

And it was revealed unto him by the Holy Ghost, that he should not see death, before he had seen the Lord's Christ.

And he came by the Spirit into the temple: and when the parents brought in the child Jesus, to do for him after the custom of the law,

Then took he him up in his arms, and blessed God, and said,

Lord [*despotes*[13]—an absolute ruler, master, or lord], now lettest thou thy servant [*doulos*[14]—slave, bondman] depart in peace, according to thy word.

Simeon's references to the Holy Ghost, the Spirit, God, the Lord, and Christ are fairly standard. They refer to the relationship between a person and his or her God. However, in verse 29 the word translated as "Lord" (*despotes*) is different than the usual word used to refer to "the Lord God" (*kyrios*). *Despotes* is more typically used when referring to the master of a slave.[15] And, consistent with this beginning, the Greek word translated as "servant" (*doulos*) continues this theme by making reference to a slave or bondman. What the modern reader sees as *Lord* and *servant* can be useful, but it is probably different than what was originally intended. Luke's use of *despotes* and *doulos* clearly implies the relationship between master and slave, not God and man.

Another example stems from KJV use of the word *handmaid*. In the KJV, at least nine Greek words are translated as "servant." But in contrast, only one word is translated as "handmaid": *doule.*[16] So Mary's reply to Gabriel at the Annunciation could have been: "Behold the [slave girl] of the Lord."[17] Her testimony to Elizabeth would have likely been similarly themed: "And my spirit hath rejoiced in God my Saviour for he hath regarded the low estate of his [slave girl], for, behold, from henceforth all generations shall call me blessed."[18]

This nuance of translation significantly alters the messages of the parable of the prodigal son, the account of Mary's call to be the mother of the Lord, and the powerful witness of Simeon. The impact of this change is individualized, but the new perspective certainly heightens the emotion and power of the stories. And considering the passages in the context of the ancient Mediterranean world, a one-word change from *servant* to *slave* dramatically alters the nature of the relationships involved. The relationship of servant and master is worlds apart from the relationship of slave and master. This perspective can influence the nature of our relationship with the Lord as we study the scriptures.

It could be said that the three examples provided above represent a larger meta-theme in the Gospel of Luke. Was Luke trying to liken the relationship between man and God to the relationship of a slave and master to teach us about true conversion to the gospel? These are certainly not Luke's only teachings that could develop and strengthen such a theme. However, this is a metaphor that is not limited to the writings of "the beloved physician."[19] The teachings of Paul are rife with metaphors of the Saints as slaves of Christ. Since Luke spent many years with Paul, there was undoubtedly some cross-pollination of ideas between the two. In fact, it would not be a big surprise if Luke's iteration of this ideology found its origins in the teachings of Paul or his Epistles, which pre-dated the Gospel of Luke and the Acts of the Apostles.[20]

In reality, the "slave of God" metaphor isn't simply Pauline or Lukan in its scope. It is discernable in the writings of most of the authors of the New Testament. Rather than being a soft-spoken theme in Luke's Gospel, the notion of the Saints submitting themselves to become slaves of God is found throughout the New Testament. In these writings, we find that this concept is developed into a more cohesive and poignant message and broadcast as a core teaching of the early Church. As such, it helped the Saints define their relationship to God after conversion and turn away from their worship of idols or the Law of Moses. To us, these teachings are therefore no less valuable in understanding our role as Latter-day Saints in God's Church.

New Testament (Greek) for *Servant*[21]

Word	Strong's Number	Definition
Diakonos	1249	Someone who executes the commands of another (such as a servant or even waiter), especially a master, minister, or king; or a deacon, one who—by virtue of the office assigned them—cares for the poor and has charge of distributing the money collected for them.
Doulos	1401	A slave, bondman, attendant, or servant (man of servile condition); or it could be a metaphor for a person who gives himself or herself up to another's will (those whose service is used by Christ in extending and advancing His cause among men); or it could mean being devoted to another to the disregard of one's own interests.

Douloo	1402	To make a slave of, reduce to bondage; or it could be a metaphor for giving yourself to another's needs, becoming a bondman.
Therapon	2324	A servant or attendant of God (spoken of Moses discharging the duties that were committed to him by God).
Misthios	3407	Employed for hire; hired.
Misthotos	3411	Someone who is hired; a hireling.
Oiketes	3610	Someone who lives in the same house as another, who is under the authority of the same householder; or a domestic servant.
Pais	3816	A child, boy or girl; also could mean a servant or slave, especially for royalty.
Hyperetes	5257	A servant, one who serves with his or her hands; anyone who aids another in any work (such as an assistant to a king or preacher of the gospel).

Chapter 2: Slavery in the Roman World

In attempting to understand the metaphor of the Saints as slaves of God, we must first understand the nature of slavery in the Roman world because it was the dominant power at the time.

Slavery and Social Status

The ancient, first-century Mediterranean world was obviously quite different from our own. Social status was an ever-present reality that divided people into a small fraction of ultra-wealthy rulers, a relatively small aristocratic class (patricians and equestrians in ancient Rome) whose wealth and access to the patronage of the ruling class ensured continued prosperity, and immense throngs of commoners who lived hand-to-mouth on a daily basis.

A couple powerful individuals dominated the ruling class of most societies. Their incredible wealth was generally a means to attain office; the office was a means to maintain their wealth. These leaders often used their wealth to buy influence among their peers or to launch military (in Rome and Hellenized states) or religious (in Israel) careers that would promote their social stature and open doors of political and economic opportunity. In ancient Rome, war and successful military leadership were ways to acquire great wealth and class advancement, often through looting and enslavement of prisoners. It was the best way to fast-track political aspirations. Political office was another way to ensure continued wealth and social stature.

The Judaic world of the Second Temple period (516 BC to AD 70) had similar strategies that were at play. Though under heavy Roman rule, the potential for high religious office was sought and bought by the ambitious because of the power it had over the people. These offices generally consisted of high priests, priests, scribes, and elders.[22] These few had tremendous influence over Judean culture and society. The highest offices, such as the high priest, often held nearly absolute power over the people they ruled. Theirs would be a life of undisputed privilege.

The Pharisees, so commonly encountered in the New Testament, often heralded from the lower and middle Judean classes. According to Josephus,[23] they generally enjoyed populist support from the people. They resisted Hellenization and clung to their heritage as Jews.[24] Their sphere of influence was rather broadly based because it centered on the synagogue and the written law. Along with the Sadducees, they had some degree of representation on the Sanhedrin, but this institution had a largely symbolic role during the period of Roman rule.[25]

The Sadducees were on the upper echelon of social and economic strata in Judean society.[26] They were ocassionally referred to as Herodians[27] because of their rise to power during the Herodian Dynasty.[28] Though lacking the populous support the Pharisees had, Sadducean control over the temple, religious feasts, and temple sacrifices put them in a position of immense power. The temple so dominated Jewish life that to control it was to control the fabric of Judean society. Jerusalem was the center of the Sadducean power base because of the temple. The Sadducees traced their authority through priestly privilege, lineage, and traditions in the Torah; they rejected the "tradition of the fathers," which was avowed by the Pharisees.[29] Though they were religiously conservative, they embraced Hellenism and were willing to work with the Roman authorities in order to maintain their power and influence. Accordingly, the Sadducees had a reputation for corruption.[30] These differences frequently put Sadducees and Pharisees in conflict with one another.[31]

Though not all priests were Sadducees, high-ranking Sadducean families used religious offices to create strangleholds on the political and economic privileges that they enjoyed.[32] The house of Hanan, son of Seth, exemplified this dominance in Christ's time. Hanan was better known as Annas, the high priest in the writings of Luke and John.[33] His power gave him a virtual monopoly on the all-important office of high priest, passing it on to five sons and finally his son-in-law, Caiaphas.[34]

In contrast to the small ruling class of Roman society, there were throngs of poor, dispossessed people who had to eke out a subsistence existence as farmers, tradesmen, or merchants. The middle class that dominates our modern society was largely absent. Each man, and his family, was one mishap—be it illness, injury, drought, or eviction—away from disaster. The only social security of the day was within the extended family. Failing this, the unfortunate were left to beg for alms in the street, to turn to crime, or to live as an indentured servant.

If this kind of abject poverty was considered to be the lowest rung on the social status ladder, then slavery was a state devoid of any honor or status whatsoever. The prevalent attitude about slavery was that it was so degrading and socially deplorable that it actually transformed the slave into a person who was not only without any social status, but also without morals. Free persons looked upon the possibility of enslavement with great horror. To call someone a slave was deeply offensive and a degrading epithet. Euripedes wrote, "If there is aught that causes slaves to blush, it is the name."[35] Though slaves were still considered to be human beings, they were not really considered to be *persons*.

Biases against slaves as being dishonest and untrustworthy were pervasive. There was a presumption that a slave was lazy, unscrupulous, and an opportunist criminal. The Roman perception was that, given the opportunity, a slave would defraud his master by slothfulness, feigned illness, sabotage, rising up in rebellion, or running away. Because of these perceptions, extremely harsh laws were enacted that enabled the punishment of problem slaves, runaway slaves, or slaves who physically assaulted their masters. For example, if a slave murdered his master, all the slaves of the household were put to death because they failed in their duty to protect their master.[36]

Slaves as Property

Slaves were considered the property of their masters and were called *res mancipi*, giving them the same legal status as cattle and property. Numerous ancient sources described slaves not as persons, but as *ta somata doulika*, or slave bodies.[37] As such, they were bought and sold at the slave market in the same manner as livestock. An unskilled adult male slave would cost between five to six hundred denarii[38] and a skilled slave as much as two thousand denarii.[39] And as was the case with livestock, slaves were sometimes branded to indicate their slave status, or they were fitted with a permanent metal collar that indicated their name, along with the name of their owner.[40]

A slave had no rights and could not own any personal property.[41] All extant family ties prior to enslavement were immediately dissolved, and a slave could not legally marry[42] or have legitimate children. Any children born to slaves were born into slavery and were considered the property of the master, just like with livestock. As a result, they could expect no guarantee that their family or personal relationships would be respected or honored by their masters.[43]

Becoming enslaved was literally a state of living death. "The slave is one who has figuratively died at the hands of his or her master, but continues to exist, for the benefit of the master alone, in a state of social death."[44] For example, if a Roman soldier were captured in battle (and thereby became the slave of his captor), he was considered dead in a legal sense, and his wife was a widow and his children were fatherless.

Familial ties were immediately severed upon entering into slavery. In essence, slaves became part of the master's family, though they did not enjoy the benefits of being family beyond basic food and shelter. Slaves had no right to control any aspects of their lives, including their bodies. The bottom-line reality of slavery was the absence of the slave's free will.

Existing in a state of total dependency and powerlessness, slaves were molded to assimilate their master's goals, agenda, and values. Good slaves loved and served their masters and accepted their lot in life. In so doing, they hoped for better treatment. The ultimate goal would have likely been to one day be granted freedom. Bad slaves frequently faced harsh treatment and incessant psychological abuse that were designed to break and pacify them. The recalcitrant were rapidly disposed of because of their perceived threat in destabilizing the family and having a corrupting influence on other slaves.

Sources of Slavery[45]

Keith Bradley estimated that between 50 BC and AD 150, around 500,000 new slaves were needed every year for the entire Roman Empire.[46] At this time, it's been estimated that on the Italian peninsula alone there were between two and three million slaves, or between 33 percent and 40 percent of the entire population.[47] The numbers are staggering and would have required an elaborate logistical system of procurement and distribution for the slave trade. It also necessitated an elaborate set of laws.

Some slaves were born free and fell into bondage as a result of war and conquest. In fact, a rather significant number of slaves came from war. To the victor went the spoils, which meant everything. That is one of the primary reasons behind Rome's state of perpetual warfare over its history: the wages of war were enormous. War plunders obviously included gold, silver, and natural resources. After the second century BC, the greatest collections of Greek art were not found in Greece, but rather in Rome as a result of their immense plunder. Less obvious to us were the riches brought by the capture of slaves. In fact, quests for slaves were often a driving force behind Rome's warmongering and expansionist tendencies. It was customary for the victors to execute large numbers of prisoners who had been taken in battle—but only rarely did they execute all of the prisoners. The spared were taken as slaves. The women, children, and non-combatant men were also taken as slaves. For example, the conquest of the Greek city-states in the second century BC saw the peninsula pillaged and depopulated as hundreds of thousands were taken into slavery and transported from there to Rome.

War was not the only source of slaves. Piracy and kidnapping were important sources of slaves for the slave trade. This was especially true of the seas around Syracuse on the Sicilian coast, where pirates went largely unchallenged. It's no wonder the crimes of piracy and banditry were so generally abhorred and aggressively punished during ancient times.[48] The threat of kidnapping and enslavement at the hands of pirates was quite real to any traveler, irrespective of social station. As a boy, even Julius Caesar found himself kidnapped by Cilician pirates and held for ransom.[49]

Another source of slavery was the exposure or abandonment of unwanted newborn children.[50] Anyone who took in foundlings had the right to consider them as slaves. Slavery could also occur as a result of being unable to pay a debt. The creditor could then sell the debtor into slavery for a period of time. Some people, utterly destitute, would sell themselves into slavery for the security of knowing they would be fed and clothed.

Those who were born into slavery were called *vernae*. The status of the slave followed that of the slave's mother—even if the father was not a slave. In fact, the law did not recognize a slave as having a father—even if paternity was obvious.[51] These home-born slaves had slightly more social acceptance than freeborn slaves. Nevertheless, their relative advantage on the social strata of home-born slaves did not transcend their bondage. They were every bit as powerless as the lowliest slave in the household.

Slavery in Roman Society

A poor Roman citizen would have one or two slaves while nobles owned perhaps four to ten slaves. The number of slaves owned was directly proportional to wealth and social stature. The senatorial class could easily employ one to two dozen urban slaves and maybe even hundreds on country estates to farm the land and rear their livestock. Caesar's household could number up to 20,000 slaves and freedmen in various servile, domestic, or administrative capacities, as well as for public works throughout the Empire.

Slaves occupied nearly every conceivable job.[52] Upper-class Roman households would have had a number of slaves who attended to domestic duties, prepared and served meals, maintained the home and grounds, and served as litter-bearers and attendants. It was fashionable to have Greek-born slaves who served as teachers, doctors, secretaries, or financial administrators. The ultra-wealthy would have had a slave for every conceivable task, no matter how seemingly esoteric. Livia, wife of Augustus, took the specialization of her slaves to new levels. Among her numerous slaves, she counted a *purpuris* (slave in charge of purple garments), an *ad unguenta* (slave in charge of perfumed oils), a *capsarius* (clothes folder), a *rogator* (issuer of invitations), and a *delicium* (pet child).[53]

The utilization of slaves in urban settings was diverse: shopkeepers, prostitutes, water bearers, street cleaners, undertakers, messengers, bodyguards—the list is endless. Slaves were employed by the state to manage public baths, maintain temples, or even function as civic administrators. Likewise, slaves were often used as tradesmen, barbers, craftsmen, or artisans. In short, slavery punctuated virtually every level of society in the Roman world.

Rural slaves (*familia rustica*) seemed to endure much harder lives than their urban counterparts (*familia urbana*) and occupied a lower social status among the servile population. The majority of rural slaves attended to the fields and flocks and rural estates of wealthy families. Similar degrees of specialization could occur with rural slaves. As almost a rule, they had long hours, meager rations, and poor living conditions. The most horrific of all were slaves consigned to work chained to an oar in a galley or toiling away in the mines. The living conditions of these slaves were utterly inhuman. Those fated to such tasks were quite literally worked to death and tossed aside like a spent battery.

Abuse and Punishment of Slaves

Roman law evolved to offer slaves some protections from the more extreme abuses of their masters. But this was little consolation in the real world of a slave. Masters had complete control over not only quality of life, but also control over life and death. Martin Hengel (1926–2009), a German religious historian, extensively documented examples of the kinds of abuses a slave could be subjected to at the hands of his or her master. He quotes Juvenal in showing that a slave could be crucified on a whim if the matron of the house was having a bad day (Juvenal, *Satire,* 6.219).[54] Horace, a Roman poet who lived at the time of Augustus, vigorously criticized the fact that a master could crucify one of his young domestic slaves for tasting the remains of the fish soup as the slave was cleaning up the dishes after dinner (Horace, *Satires,* Book 1, Satire III).[55] Hengel also cites Seneca the Elder's legal arguments against Parrhasius, an Athenian painter. Parrhasius purchased an older man, who was a prisoner of war, from a slave trader, and then tortured him to death while using him as a model for his painting of Prometheus in the Temple of Minerva (Seneca, *Controversiae* 10.5).[56]

Hengel elaborately outlined crucifixion as "the slaves' punishment" (*servile supplicium*) in Roman society.[57] For the modern Christian, we have a tendency to associate crucifixion with the death of Jesus Christ in an almost exclusive fashion. In reality, crucifixion was the form of execution reserved for rebellious slaves, pirates, and traitors—but mostly it was used on slaves. It was the epitome of a cruel, painful, and humiliating death and therefore considered fitting for only the most despised human condition. It served as a potent deterrent to keep the large slave population of Roman Empire in subjection.[58] Rome used it with great frequency and created public places for the crucifixion of slaves in every major city within the Empire. Hengel quoted Juvenal (Juvenal, *Satire* 14.77), saying that "the vulture hurries from dead cattle and dogs and crosses to bring some of the carrion to her offspring." He treated the matter so casually to make the observation scarcely worth noting.

For most slaves, the threat of death by crucifixion was a powerful deterrent to rising up against their masters. Of equal importance in their subjection and pacification was the day-to-day treatment that they received at the hands of their masters. Slaves were frequently the victims of sexual abuse by their masters.[59] It was considered normal for a master to use a slave for his sexual gratification. Similarly, a master had complete control over informal slave unions that were used to reward, punish, or just increase the population of the family's slaves.

A slave had to live in constant state of abuse at his or her master's hands.[60] They were regularly beaten or whipped for even the slightest offense. In the second century AD, the physician Galen of Pergamum (circa AD 130–200) wrote up a treatise entitled *On the Passions and Errors of the Soul*, in which he counseled men to control their irascible nature. In chilling detail, he chronicled the tendency of masters to bite their slaves (his own mother), hit them with their fists, or gouge their eyes out. He qualified this behavior as being problematic, but less so than that of striking doors, stones, or other inanimate objects. Emperor Hadrian blinded one of his slaves in a fit of rage by stabbing his eye with a stylus. One of Galen's friends struck two of his slaves on the top of their heads with the narrow end of a sheathed sword—all for not immediately knowing where his luggage was. According to Galen, his folly was in not using the broad side of the scabbard. His impetuousness had inflicted bodily injury to the slaves and necessitated medical treatment to save their lives. Even more concerning to Galen was the all-too-frequent scenario of the master bruising a tendon in his hand or foot as a result. Injuries to the master were so unnecessary. "They could have waited a little while, he said, and used a rod or whip to inflict as many blows as they wished and to accomplish the act with reflection."[61] From his youth, Galen placed an injunction on himself to never strike a slave with his hand.

Any kind of punishment deemed appropriate by the master was permitted, and we are left with the impression that, for most slaves, they were subjected to constant threats of beatings, punctuated with frequent instances of actual abuse. So institutionalized was the physical punishment of slaves that, in Rome, it could actually be hired out to professional torturers[62] who were known as *manceps.*[63] This was a group of enterprising undertakers who would, for a fixed price, provide all forms of punishment to slaves. Punishments typically consisted of floggings, burnings (by applying boiling pitch, metal plates, or flaming torches), or racking on devices designed to separate a person limb from limb. In cases where legal testimony of a slave was to be used as evidence in a court of law, torture was a prerequisite for the testimony to be admissible. In fact, the court actually provided the necessary facilities for the torture of slaves, much as it would provide a bailiff or court stenographer today.

As a result of harsh treatment, under-nourishment, and immensely hard work and neglect, many slaves developed significant ailments and deformities over time. As a result, slaves (in a very literal sense) wore out their bodies in the service of their masters. What use was a slave who was blind, lame, or unable to work? When age, infirmity, or disease made them unable to remain profitable, they faced prospects of an accelerated decline because of disease, abuse, and ever-greater neglect. In the worst cases, masters would offer them their freedom so as to be spared the responsibility for their maintenance and support. In such cases, their lifelong desire came on the wings of a lonely death.

Seneca the Younger wrote extensively about Roman injustices and abuses toward their slaves in his epistle, "On Master and Slave." He encouraged masters to treat slaves with dignity and basic kindness, but he never suggested that owning of slaves in the first place was in any way inappropriate.[64] It seems no one could envision a world without it—in fact, it was considered a necessity of life, as it was then known. There are many ancient writings on slavery as an institution or on legal ramifications of slavery, proper treatment of slaves, and slave rights, but none of these ever went so far as to consider the abolition of slavery. Even the writings of early Church leaders seem to accept the institution of slavery as a reality of everyday life.

Manumission

The stoic Dio Chrysostum wrote, "Men desire above all things to be free."[65] For a slave, the ultimate hope was freedom. Manumission was the process whereby a slave was given that.[66] Formal manumission was an officially recognized legal action that had to be recorded by the civil magistrate because it simultaneously granted the former slave Roman citizenship. Informal manumission may have simply been a letter of emancipation, a private ceremony in which a slave's freedom was granted in front of witnesses. The latter may have been more common because it did not require the payment of a manumission tax. Either way, the former master would usually provide the freed slave with a grant of support to start a business or with a small plot of land to farm.

The hope of manumission was simply another tool by which a slave owner could increase the profitability of his investment. It was the ultimate carrot that could be used to motivate the faithful service of a slave. Realistically, the prospects of manumission were negligible for rural slaves and nonexistent for mine or galley slaves. Urban slaves had a realistic prospect of earning or buying their freedom by their thirties,[67] or after ten to twenty years of service.[68] Martin suggested that in the Greek east, it could cost a slave four hundred drachmae to purchase his or her freedom, a sum of money sufficient to sustain a peasant family for over three years.[69]

Following manumission, former slaves were known as freedmen. In most cases, they continued as a patron of their former master. As such, they remained in a dependent state on their former master and often continued to collaborate in economic activities. Some freedmen continued in the same capacity as they had as slaves—albeit with a far greater sense of dignity. Even if their daily toils had not changed measurably, the difference between being freedmen and being slaves meant everything. It is one of the greatest metaphors for resurrection that has ever existed. A man, having existed in a state of living death, was now alive once more. Whereas life as a slave meant he had no control, no self-determination, and no free will, he was now granted all of these in an instant.

Conclusion

It is important to acknowledge that our understanding of slavery in the ancient world is incomplete, told from every perspective *except* that of the slave. But it is complete enough to realize the unspeakable suffering and horror associated with life as a slave. In contrast, slavery was as common a phenomenon in the first-century Church as beasts of burden were to the pioneers or as automobiles are to us. These early Saints would've known intimately the pitiful state of a slave and could only envision their own enslavement in their nightmares. Yet with this understanding, we can begin to understand the revolutionary teaching of the Christian religion in espousing a doctrine of willful enslavement to God as a metaphor of conversion.

Chapter 3: Slavery as a Theme in the Teachings of Jesus Christ

Jesus Christ was, without doubt, the greatest teacher that the world has ever known. As a teacher, His ability to use the ordinary and mundane events of daily life as profound teaching moments was unsurpassed. Whether it was a laborer in a field, a woman who was drawing water from a well, or the sight of a sparrow on a branch, He found ways to use a given event as an unforgettable teaching moment that directed people's thoughts to God.

Slavery as a subject in the teachings of Jesus Christ is surprisingly common. In some instances, it was probably used as a teaching moment, much as He would have used a sparrow or the water at the well or a laborer in the field. Yet there are many instances in which He used the images and emotions of slavery in a much more deliberate manner. Undoubtedly, slavery existed as an everyday reality in His time. All Jews were intimately aware of their history of captivity and deliverance in Egypt, in Babylon, and even in their own lands over continual wars and conflicts with their neighbors. Accordingly, the theme of slavery was fertile ground on which the Savior could plant His seeds.

Slavery in Ancient Hebrew Law

The Hebrew word *'ebed,*[70] though generally translated as "servant," means "slave" or "bondman." It is first used in the Old Testament in Genesis 9 to describe Caanan's curse.[71] There are extensive descriptions of Abram being a slave owner. For example, he mustered 318 fighting men from home-born slaves[72] in order to save his nephew Lot from captivity. Following Abram's liberation of Lot, the captives were then given as slaves to the king of Sodom. This custom of taking people captive after conquest in war continued through the history of the Israelite conflict. These and other examples abound to the extent that there can be no dispute about the institution of slavery being a routine part of Jewish life from the earliest times.

Specific laws for Jewish slave owners[73] were established and codified in the law of Moses.[74] Jewish law granted asylum to runaway slaves.[75] Non-Jews could be treated as chattel and thus owned as slaves in the Greco-Roman tradition. Jewish slaves were treated as hired hands[76] and could not be used for sexual exploitation,[77] as was common with slavery in general. Jewish law dictated that a Jew's soul could not be owned by anyone other than Jehovah because they were redeemed from slavery in Egypt.[78] Jews were under divine directive to treat their slaves with kindness.[79] Enslaved fellow Jews were to be liberated with an inheritance during the Jubilee year,[80] or after six years of being a slave.[81] Finally, there was special dispensation given to enslaved Jews who allowed for their purchase and liberation by a kinsman redeemer (*ga'al*).[82]

There is some debate as to the degree that Jewish slavery differed from slavery in the ancient Mediterranean during Greco-Roman times. Authors have contended that Roman family law and local custom had a greater day-to-day impact on the operational aspects of slavery than did rabbinic teachings of Mosaic law. They argue that the forms and structures of Jewish slavery were similar to the forms of slavery of other peoples living in the eastern Roman Empire.[83]

Slavery in Ancient Hebrew Doctrine

From a theological perspective, the Lord's prophet is often referred to as a slave of God in the Old Testament. Moses, in acknowledging his inadequacies before the Lord, referred to himself as the Lord's slave.[84] The theme of the prophet being the slave of God continued from Moses[85] to include others such as Samuel,[86] Joshua,[87] Isaiah,[88] Daniel,[89] the prophets in general,[90] King David,[91] and the Messiah.[92] The continuation of this theme in the prophets of the New Testament will be addressed later in this book.

Doctrinally, the tradition of the Israelites being the slaves of God finds its origins early in the Hebraic tradition. The metaphor of Moses being Jehovah's slave struck a resonant chord with the Hebrew people, having just experienced miraculous deliverance from their bondage of Egypt. "For unto me the children of Israel are servants [*'ebed*]; they are my servants [*'ebed*] whom I brought forth out of the land of Egypt: I am the Lord your God" (Leviticus 25:55).

The doctrine expanded from the concept of Moses as God's slave to the people as God's slaves.[93] I. A. H. Combes eloquently summarized this doctrine: "Those who worship God are, in the Hebrew mind, God's slaves, and those who worship other gods and idols are likewise slaves of these. The Hellenistic tradition, on the other hand, shows no sign of such communal, literal slavery."[94]

Slavery in the Teachings of Jesus Christ

There is evidence that Mary, mother of the Lord, viewed herself as a slave of God, based on her referring to herself as "the handmaid of the Lord."[95] Perhaps it was His mother who first taught Jesus the metaphor that likened a Jew to a *slave* of Jehovah. There can be no doubt that this theme resonated with Jesus as He grew in wisdom and stature[96] and became conversant with the esteemed teachers of His day. The proof for this resonance was His extensive use of the images and emotions of slavery in His parables and other teachings.[97] Depending how you define a parable, just about half of the Savior's parables are peopled with slaves.[98] Slavery is so central to the parables and teachings of Jesus that some scholars have actually suggested Jesus was a former slave.[99]

Several of Jesus's parables refer to slavery in an almost incidental manner. For example, in the first chapter of this book we reviewed the parable of the prodigal son, which introduces slavery without any doctrinal overtones about our enslavement to God. However, the parable is instructive about the social institution of slavery. For example, the prodigal son descended so low that he considered the fate of his father's slaves better than his own. It also depicts the utterly servile nature of slaves, as they have to dress the prodigal son. Finally, it is symbolic of God's acceptance of us as His prodigal children when we return to Him in humility.

Other parables develop the Old Testament theme of the prophet being the slave of Jehovah. The parable of the wedding guests sees the slaves of the master rejected[100] and even beaten and killed[101] when they pass out invitations to a great wedding feast. This is a great lesson about pride. The master represents God and His slaves represent His prophets. Those invited have their various excuses, but ultimately they reject the invitation. In rejecting the prophets and their invitation, the guests reject God and therefore suffer His judgments and are destroyed. By contrast, the humble and the destitute accept the invitation and are invited into the feast.

This theme is further developed and expanded in the parable of the wicked husbandmen.[102] Once again, the slaves of the lord of the vineyard are beaten, wounded, and sent away. The lord sends his son, expecting that he will be honored and received. Yet the husbandmen kill the son of the lord of the vineyard in an attempt to claim the vineyard as their own. This parable builds upon the aforementioned theological foundation that viewed the prophets as the slaves of God and pointed to their role in preceding the Messiah. It also struck a tender chord with the chief priests and scribes who sought to kill Jesus after hearing it.

Additional parables of Jesus all clearly reinforce the teaching that every man was likewise enslaved to God. As discussed in the second chapter of this book, slaves could live in a semi-autonomous fashion as client-patrons of their masters and have a wife and children.[103] These business ventures often provided the master with a portion of the revenues from the business. If the slave were unprofitable or did not meet his financial obligations to the master, the business could be foreclosed or taken over and the master could sell the slave's wife or children to pay his debts. The parable of the unforgiving servant[104] is that of a slave with an enormous debt to the king. He is threatened with the enslavement of his wife and children. He begs for mercy and is given more time to pay the debt. The pardoned slave then goes out and finds a poor man who owes him a trivial debt, refuses to forgive him, and casts him in debtor's prison. Ultimately, the king recognizes this man's unforgiving nature when he is in such desperate need of mercy himself and thus decides to have the unmerciful slave punished and delivered to the tormentors.[105]

Certainly this parable is more about forgiveness than it is about slavery. But who can doubt that Jesus was attempting to secondarily reinforce the reality of our own enslavement and indebtedness to the King of Kings?

Though more complex in its construct, a similar message is given in John when Jesus taught His followers that "the truth shall make you free."[106] The mere suggestion that a man was not free was to suggest him a slave. In the first century AD, to liken a person to a slave was deeply offensive. With this teaching, Jesus was certainly able to get the attention of His audience. He taught that we all have been enslaved either to sin or to God as a consequence of His redemption of us. As a result, a slave was redeemed from sin to become the property of a new master: God.

Jesus taught a related principle using the metaphor of slavery in Luke 16:13: "No servant can serve two masters: for either he will hate the one, and love the other; or else he will hold to the one, and despise the other. Ye cannot serve God and mammon." Parallel accounts are found in Matthew 6:24 and 3 Nephi 13:24, which seems to indicate the great importance of this teaching in the doctrine of Jesus Christ. The only way a slave could win the affection of his master was through absolute obedience. A slave couldn't satisfy the demands of two masters with different goals. Perfect devotion to one would be tantamount to betrayal of the other. Any attempts to serve both simultaneously would make him unfaithful for giving less than his complete devotion. What better metaphor than a slave could be used to illustrate the dichotomy of choice we all face in the placement of our loyalties?

An initial review of the parable of the wheat and the tares[107] seems to refer to slaves indirectly as well. Having discovered tares in the field, the slaves come to the master for advice. Their gut instincts about how to deal with the tares were completely wrong. As they seek the master's help, they are instructed and counseled on how to solve the problem. With the assistance of the master—who is wiser and more experienced—they can see the problem in a clearer context and wider perspective. The master teaches them not only what to do, but when to do it. Though seemingly tangential in its use of slavery to teach, this parable emphasizes that we as slaves of God must look to Him for counsel, direction, and perspective to understand and overcome the obstacles we will face in life.

The parable of the talents[108] builds on the teachings of Isaiah, which portray Jehovah as a kind and generous master[109] to those slaves who serve and love Him. It reaffirms God's loving devotion to His faithful servants and the weighty repercussions that await those who are openly rebellious. In this parable, a wealthy man appoints stewardships to his slaves—each according to their several abilities—while he is traveling abroad.

To the disciples who heard the parable from Jesus, it would have been clear that the slaves in this parable weren't regular domestic slaves. For us, the implication is not obvious until we consider the size of the investment the master entrusted to his slaves. Stewardships of five, three, and one talents were fantastic sums of money. A talent was the equivalent of six thousand denarii.[110] Typical wages for a day's labor was one denarius. In other words, it would take a man over nineteen years, working six days a week, to earn one talent. These stewardships were therefore sufficiently large to discern that the slaves were not simple domestics, but rather highly competent and trusted administrators who managed the master's affairs. Such practices were commonplace in the Roman Empire because slaves routinely functioned as financial administrators, treasurers, landlords, and in other high-level positions under Caesar and other elite Roman families.[111]

The expectation is established that the slaves would be diligent with this sizable investment and generate a profit for their master.[112] The reaction of the master when he comes to make a reckoning with his slaves is the whole point of the parable. But in making this point, we must remember that the slaves in this instance were hand-selected, highly trusted, and commissioned according to their abilities. Much had been given and much was expected.[113] To the faithful, profitable slave, the master praises, "Well done, good and faithful slave." Their faithfulness was richly rewarded with an appointment over enormous worldly holdings and also joy of their master. It was a step toward their ultimate manumission that could be expected if they stayed faithful.

To the unfaithful and unprofitable slave, the master was austere and exacting. This slave had betrayed the master's trust, shirked his duty as he made no effort to attend to his stewardship. His failures are better thought of as open rebellion because a minimal effort would have yielded a 4–8 percent return through the moneychangers or bankers.[114] The master's reaction to the wicked slave was extremely harsh. That which he had was taken from him and he was cast out of the palace to await punishment at the hands of the *manceps* (professional torturers).

Luke's account of the parable of the pounds[115] has many elements in common with the parable of the talents. However, several important differences remain. In this parable, the master is a wealthy nobleman who is traveling abroad so he may inherit a kingdom. It is reminiscent of the events that transpired after the death of Herod the Great, when his son, Archaelaus, traveled to Rome to formally inherit his kingdom.[116] The parable was likely a strategy to tie parabolic teaching to current events that would have been obvious to the people.

In this parable, the nobleman calls ten slaves and gives one minas to each of them with instructions to occupy (*pragmateuomai*, meaning carry on a business, possibly of a banker or trader[117]) until he returns. While abroad, some citizens complained against their would-be king, but to no avail (the Jews unsuccessfully petitioned Caesar[118] to not appoint Archaelaus as Herod the Great's successor).

In Matthew's account, the master gives his slaves *talents*. In Luke's account, he gives them *minas* (translated as "pounds" in KJV). Either way, these stewardships represents substantial sums of money. One minas was equal to a hundred denarii[119] and one talent was sixty minas. In Luke's account, the stewardships represented the equivalent of three months' salary. Though substantially smaller than the parable of the talents, it still conveys the reality that the master had entrusted his money to hand-selected slaves of whom he had great trust and high expectations. When the rewards are presented, the faithful are given authority over cities instead of minas. The wicked slave loses everything and the citizens that tried to depose him are slaughtered.[120]

Luke's parable of the minas also evokes images of the wickedness and cruelty of Archaelaus and the just judgments of God in dealing with subjects or slaves who willfully disobeyed and rose up against authority. In both instances, the king has total authority; those who oppose or rise up in defiance can expect swift and austere punishment. Yet for the faithful, things go quite well.

The Gospel of Luke juxtaposes two parables to contrast the master's response to faithful slaves[121] with their wicked slave overseer.[122] The parable of the faithful slaves plays off the parable of the ten virgins.

The exact time of the return of their lord from the wedding is unknown but imminent. The faithful slave is expected to be dressed and ready to serve, irrespective of the hour. When his master knocks and finds him ready, he is blessed beyond expectation. In an instant, the slave becomes the master and the master becomes the slave. His lord puts on work clothes, invites the slave to recline, and serves him a feast.

The parable is a clear foreshadowing of Christ's Second Coming, the timing of which is unknown but imminent. It emphasizes that a faithful slave must be vigilant. He is never able to let down his guard or completely rest. He must always be ready to serve his master at any hour and in any way. When he is found faithful at the coming of the master, he is blessed beyond his wildest expectations.

In the parable of the overseer, Jesus contrasted the faithful slaves of the household with the wickedness of the slave who had been made their overseer. It is assumed that the other slaves cannot be trusted to work, supervise themselves, ration their food, and so on while the master is away. The master has handpicked the overseer. In him, the master places greater trust and much higher expectations because he "knew his lord's will." A central element of this parable is the overseer's prior wisdom and faithfulness.[123] Luke spoke of him when saying, "For unto whomsoever much is given, of him shall be much required: and to whom men have committed much, of him they will ask the more" (Luke 12:48).

But in spite of his position of trust and his understanding of the responsibilities, the overseer willfully neglects his duty. He is abusive to those in his care, irresponsible, and self-serving. With the sudden return of the master, his procrastination and his flagrant defiance are apparent. His disobedience promotes the disobedience of his fellow slaves, for which they are punished. But because their transgressions were not premeditated, their punishments are mild by comparison. The overseer is beaten with many stripes whereas the slaves who were ignorant are beaten with a few stripes. In the end, the overseer receives a punishment that is as horrible in degree as the blessings of the faithful slaves are great. After being brutally scourged, he is cut into pieces and counted with the nonbelievers.

The contrast of the severity of the punishments of the guilty with their level of understanding is critical to understand. The motive behind the transgression determines the severity of the punishment. Likewise, the motive behind the obedience determines the richness of the reward. Faithfulness is more than the completion of an assigned task. It implies willful obedience and loving devotion to the master.

Luke's parable of the farmer's slaves[124] illustrates that successful completion of a task is not the same thing as faithful obedience. The farmer's slaves labored all day in the fields. Upon their return in the evening, their reward was to begin their domestic chores and prepare the master's meal. We have no indication that they were disobedient or did not complete their assigned duties of the day. Yet their lack of reward was notably absent. No "well done, good slave" accolades awaited them; no "recline and let me serve you" surprises greeted them.

The parable of the farmer's slaves teaches about the social strata that existed between a slave and a master. Slaves did the will and bidding of their masters without question. To question or disobey was to invoke punishment. Absolute obedience was not a matter of choice, but rather a matter of necessity and survival. Slavery was total loss of agency. Slaves worked all day in the field and then labored in the home. A slave owner would not thank them for their services any more than you would thank the microwave when it worked. It was a harsh reality, but also a teaching point for Christ. It serves to remind us that when we are obedient to the commandments of the Lord, we do not fall into the trap of thinking we are profitable.

The parables of Christ about slaves and their surrender of will are instructive. The faithful slave is willfully obedient and genuine in his or her love and devotion to the master. The wicked overseer is willfully disobedient. Their rewards sit at opposite extremes of the spectrum. In between is the obedience of the famer's slaves, which can be considered obedience by necessity. Though not deserving punishment, it merits no reward.

One of the least obvious references to slavery is in the eleventh chapter of Matthew:

Matthew 11:28–30

Come unto me, all ye that labour and are heavy laden, and I will give you rest. Take my yoke upon you, and learn of me; for I am meek and lowly in heart: and ye shall find rest unto your souls. For my yoke is easy, and my burden is light.

This is one of the most familiar sayings of Jesus Christ, and one that is central to His doctrine. Yet to us, Christ's reference to slavery in this saying is not as apparent as is would be to the people of His day. For the Jews, *yoke* (*'ol*) was a term that was symbolic of slavery and servitude. For example, Leviticus 26:13 says, "I [am] the Lord your God, which brought you forth out of the land of Egypt, that ye should not be their bondmen; and I have broken the bands of your yoke."[125] The law of Moses frequently stipulated that sacrificial animals needed to have never been subjected to the yoke to be deemed suitable for sacrificial offerings.[126]

The prophecies of Isaiah,[127] Jeremiah,[128] Ezekiel,[129] and other Old Testament prophets[130] all use *yoke* metaphorically in speaking of the captivity, bondage, and enslavement of the children of Israel. This was not limited to the Jews. To be "under the yoke" in the Roman world was to be in subjugation. Roman soldiers forced vanquished prisoners of war to pass under a symbolic yoke—an archway fashioned out of spears, symbolizing their enslavement. Thereafter, they could be taken away into slavery or killed.[131] On occasion, defeated Roman armies were also subjected to this ritual to further humiliate them.[132]

Central to the concept of being a Jew is "acceptance of the yoke of the kingdom of heaven" and "acceptance of yoke of the commandments."[133] Jewish thinking in Christ's time dictated that to keep the law of Moses was to be "under the yoke of the law," which effected the removal of "the yoke of worldly care."[134] Though our connotations are negative, Jews thought of this yoke as a great blessing. They were liberated from bitter slavery and captivity and now served a master who was loving and kind. This yoke taught them how to live and worship God. But the yoke of the law was heavy because it demanded obedience with exactness.

The invitation of the Savior to His followers to take on His yoke offered to exchange something that was good for something that was much better. Both Peter and Paul likened the yoke of the law to the yoke of bondage.[135] The yoke of Christ introduces a new master-slave relationship, with Christ as the master. The redemptive power of His Atonement made an easy yoke for those who come to learn of Him and become His slaves.

The theme of voluntarily taking on the yoke of Christ is reinforced by another saying of His: "If any [man] will come after me, let him deny himself, and take up his cross, and follow me" (Matthew 16:24). That this teaching is central to the doctrine of Christ is evidenced by its documentation on many occasions in the synoptic Gospels.[136] Just as the yoke became symbolic of slavery and servitude, so too was the cross a symbol of slavery. Though Rome used crucifixion to execute pirates and insurrectionists, it was primarily a punishment reserved for slaves.[137] The cross was therefore an image that was hopelessly entwined with slavery. The last act of the slave was to carry his cross to the place of his execution. For the Jew, both the yoke and the cross denoted enslavement. Therefore, the process of "taking up your cross" was a variant of the same theme that required followers of Jesus to voluntarily enslave themselves to Him as their master and follow His example.

A final metaphor of slavery that punctuated Christ's teachings was underscored at the Last Supper: The slave is not greater than his lord.[138] By washing the feet of the Twelve, He epitomized His teaching that the greatest disciple would be the slave of all.[139] His directive to "come follow me" was not rhetorical, but literal. He expected His followers to lose their lives in service.[140]

The washing of feet was the *sine qua non* duty of a slave. After the Last Supper, Jesus changed His clothes and "took a towel and girded himself" (John 13:4). Harris noted that the Greek word for "towel" (*lention*) denotes the apron donned by a slave when about to work.[141] This scene is reminiscent of the parable in which the lord girds himself and serves the slaves after returning from the wedding to find them waiting faithfully (Luke 12:37). It may also represent foreshadowing of the fate Jesus knew awaited Him on Golgotha.[142] Thayer's Lexicon suggests that the *lention* was additionally used to cover the nakedness of persons undergoing crucifixion.[143] Either way, it is clear that this was a ritual so strongly associated with slavery that Peter initially refused to allow Jesus to do it. But He insisted, saying without the ordinance, Peter would have no future with Him. The Lord then says:

John 13:12–17

Know ye what I have done to you? Ye call me Master and Lord: and ye say well; for so I am. If I then, your Lord and Master, have washed your feet; ye also ought to wash one another's feet. For I have given you an example, that ye should do as I have done to you. Verily,

verily, I say unto you, The servant is not greater than his lord; neither he that is sent greater than he that sent him. If ye know these things, happy are ye if ye do them.

In all that He did, Jesus Christ placed the will of His father before His own.[144] In the face of unspeakable suffering and tribulations, His response was that of a slave in demonstrating complete submission and obedience to His master: "thy will be done."[145] So it was for Peter and his companions—become a slave to others in the service of your master. In the end, the men who were once slaves of Christ become His friends.[146]

Summary

The teachings of Jesus Christ are rife with metaphors and images of slavery. Though many may have represented incidental references in teaching other lessons, there is a discernible theme that expounds on Jewish doctrine that the prophets, the Messiah, and even ordinary Jews are the slaves of the Lord. Finding ourselves in this position, we must make the decision to serve only one master: God. Christ asked us to look to Him for guidance and support in our trials, for He is wiser than we are. We have to recognize that we must be ever-ready to serve him in any way. Faithful slaves are loved and rewarded while unfaithful slaves are severely punished. What separates them in the end is willful obedience of the heart. The farmer's slaves went through the motions and, though they did not receive any punishment, they did not merit a reward.

Christ's ultimate teachings about slaves were manifest in His actions during the final days of His ministry. He taught that the master was no greater that the slave and that the disciple who would be greatest should be servant of all. At the Last Supper, He symbolized His status as God's slave in washing the feet of the Apostles while wearing the apron of a slave. He then taught them that they must follow Him and give their lives in slavery to God by serving others. His final lesson in the Garden, in the face of terror and pain, was to subject Himself to God's will and be the perfect slave.

CHAPTER 4: SLAVERY IN THE EARLY CHRISTIAN CHURCH

Christianity was born in the Roman Empire and, as a result, experienced all the realities of the Roman institution of slavery from its inception. Just as the footprint of slavery was visible in every aspect of life in the Roman Empire, so it was in the early Church.

New Testament writers speak of slavery in a nonjudgmental fashion, without challenging the institution as being right or wrong.[147] Luke in particular has frequent references to slavery in his Gospel. His Gospel champions the perspective of the down and out: women, lepers, and the infirm—but also the slave. Scholars have postulated that Luke may have been a slave himself. He had a slave's name, was from an ethnic group that was often enslaved, and had a slave's profession.[148] There are frequent examples in which Church leaders encourage slaves to be faithful and obedient to their masters, and masters to treat their slaves with dignity and kindness.[149]

And multiple instances of Christian Saints being slaves have been documented. Paul's reference[150] to some of the Corinthian Saints as "them which are of the house of Chloe" could be a reference to the "slaves of Chloe." Callistus was a bishop at Rome and an ex-slave. He became a freedman and advanced in the leadership of the Christian Church.[151]

Slaves were on equal spiritual ground with both freedmen and the freeborn persons in the eyes of the Church. Enslavement was evidently no obstacle to membership or even leadership in the Church. Early Church doctrine held that Jesus Christ was a brother of the slave as well as the free. John Chrysostum[152] was no fan of slavery: "Slavery is the fruit of covetousness, of degradation, of savagery."[153] Nevertheless, he realized the reality of the institution of slavery and that it wasn't going anywhere anytime soon. Accordingly, in reference to Ephesians 6:5–8, he taught that the converted slave "is a brother, or rather has become a brother, he has received the same (gifts), he belongs to the same body. Indeed, he is the brother not only of his own master, but even of the son of God."[154]

Another example of slavery among the early Christians is evident in the writings of Pliny the Younger. In AD 112, while he was governor of Pontus and Bithynia, Pliny reported to the Emperor Trajan on his handling of accusations brought to him about Christians, which were becoming prominent.[155]

> For many persons of every age, every rank, and also of both sexes are and will be endangered. For the contagion of this superstition has spread not only to the cities but also to the villages and farms.[156]

Some of the earliest Church communities were established in this part of Asia Minor on the shores of the Black Sea. It was no small concern to the Roman authorities that the Christian community refused to participate in the cult rituals of the state religion.[157] Pliny stated that Christians were notable for their "stubbornness and inflexible obstinacy." This was demonstrated by their refusal to recant their beliefs and curse Christ, resulting in their executions. As part of his investigations into the new religion, Pliny arranged for the torture of two female slaves who were prominent in the local Christian Church. It was his attempt to gain information about the fledgling religion using a standard method of judicial inquiry: the torture of slaves. This further documented that it was not uncommon for slaves to be numbered among members of the early Church.[158] In the end, Pliny reported, "I discovered nothing else but depraved, excessive superstition."[159]

Even as the early Saints welcomed slaves into their congregations and firmly believed slavery represented no obstacle to eternal salvation, they continued business as usual demeanor in buying and selling women and men in slavery. Likewise, they continued to employ the standard tactics of strict discipline[160] and measured rewards interspersed with threats and physical punishments to control their slaves and make them profitable. There are undoubtedly some traditions that suggest early Christians were renowned for the good treatment of their slaves and the tendency to free them.[161] This was not enough, however, to challenge the institution of slavery on anything but an isolated scale. Most scholars and historians agree that despite a few exceptions, the Roman model of slavery was largely unchallenged and unthreatened by Christianity.[162]

The Epistle of Paul to Philemon exemplifies the reality of slavery in the early Church. This was written to Philemon of Colossae while Paul was under house arrest in Rome and awaiting an appearance before Nero. Though not enjoying full freedom of movement as a result this "imprisonment,"[163] Paul had been busy with his fellow laborers, who included Mark, Luke, Demas, and others.[164] Onesimus was one of Paul's converts and been enlisted in the ministry with Paul and his brethren.[165] But Onesimus had baggage in that he was a runaway slave. As such, he had stolen from his master Philemon—namely himself—along with whatever money or property he could carry. Accordingly, Paul returned Onesimus to Philemon and thereby restored the lost *property* to its rightful owner.

Roman law demanded that a fugitive slave be reported to authorities immediately. To harbor a runaway slave was illegal and tantamount to theft. Because of his fugitive status, Onesimus was subject to any kind of punishment deemed appropriate by his master. This punishment could range from beating, scourging, branding with "F" or "FVG" (to indicate a propensity to run away), demotion in his labors, sale to a new owner, or a much worse fate.[166] It was not uncommon for fugitive slaves to be publicly tortured and crucified as a deterrent to other slaves. None of this was lost to Paul. Fitzmyer[167] suggested that *The Epistle of Paul to Philemon* represents an intercession on the part of Paul to Philemon that negated Onesimus's fugitive status by peaceably returning the slave without involving Roman authorities. Yet at no time did Paul suggest that the enslavement of Onesimus was unjust, or that he should not be returned to his master, as the law demanded.

This epistle is the loudest "between the lines" communication in scripture. Though delivered in writing rather than orally, it is a fine example of Paul's mastery of rhetoric.[168] In returning Onesimus, Paul left the matter of how to handle Onesimus to Philemon. Yet the tone of his letter leaves no doubt as to how Paul felt the situation should be handled.

Paul started by pointing out that he could speak boldly in Christ on what Philemon should do, but, in the name of love and as the aged prisoner of Jesus Christ, he does not. Using play on words, Paul concedes that Onesimus (whose name means "useful") had been "useless"[169] to Philemon. However, Paul's letter immediately goes on to emphasize that Onesimus was now "useful" to both Philemon and Paul in his ministry in Rome.[170] He would have preferred to keep Onesimus so he could minister to him in his bondage and advancing age, but not without the consent of Philemon, the rightful owner.

Paul pled on behalf of Onesimus, referring to him as his son, sent from his heart and begotten in his bonds. Ironically, Philemon was also a convert of Paul and was indebted to Paul for the salvation of his soul. Paul offers to assume the responsibility for any financial burdens stemming from Onesimus's escape. Though implied, Paul thought it unnecessary to make a direct reference to the "life for a life" nuance at play here. He hints that though Philemon was deprived of his slave for a time, it was for the higher purpose of having him back forever—as a brother. Though respectively master and slave, Philemon and Onesimus were both sons of Paul through their conversion, and therefore brothers. Furthermore, the fact that both of them were Christians made them brothers in Christ. The epistle speaks powerfully as to how the gospel can turn an apostle into a prisoner and a slave into a brother.

Paul's outline of this new fraternal relationship, combined with his expressed knowledge of Philemon's loyalty, faithfulness, and personal indebtedness, put Philemon in the position of not having much choice in the whole affair. Paul had no doubt that Philemon would exceed his expectations and welcome Onesimus as if it were Paul himself. In a final request, Paul asked that Philemon prepare lodging for him in the expectation that he would soon visit Colossae in person—and check in on Philemon and Onesimus in the process.

The Epistle of Paul to Philemon seems to be more about the slave than about the institution of slavery. For Paul and the early Church leaders, the soul was of far greater concern than the body. The notion of an earthly master of a slave was of less concern, given the reality of a "Master in heaven,"[171] to which both slave and slave owner must ultimately answer. This realization—that the souls of all men were precious in the sight of God—placed Christianity centuries ahead of the civilized world in changing its attitudes about slavery.

Though slavery in the Christian community would continue for hundreds of years, after a while it became distasteful to the Christian palate and was ultimately recognized as being inconsistent with the gospel of Jesus Christ. These attitudes about slavery began only as a small trickle of water, but they would eventually be transformed into a flood so powerful that it would wash away many of the traces of slavery from the Biblical record. In its place was a strong bias against what had been a shameful mark on human history for over a thousand years. Because of this negative bias, translators softened words like *doulos* by substituting "servant" for "slave," thereby changing the original message and obscuring its meaning.

Chapter 5: The Slavery of Sin

Slavery in the ancient world was the ultimate representation of personal disenfranchisement. Slaves had no control over any aspects of their lives and complete absence of any sort of agency or self-determination. In contrast, the master, had control over everything. The slave was often thought of as a body that was to be used however a master saw fit. This is evidenced by the fact that the word *body* (Greek *soma*)[172] was often used synonymously with *slave* in the Greco-Roman world. Many ancient documents referred to slaves not as persons, but rather counted them simply as bodies.[173]

In a fundamental sense, slavery involves absence of rights, especially the right to determine the course of their lives and the use of their energies. What the slave is denied is freedom of action and movement. A slave is unable to do what he or she wishes or go where he or she wants to go. The faculty of full choice and the power of refusal are denied.[174]

Though slavery was visible at every level of society in the ancient world, and even common in the early Christian community, only a minority of the early Christians were slaves. Yet personal enslavement to another wasn't the only way agency could be lost or surrendered. Enslavement to sin was much more worrisome for the early Church leaders than personal enslavement. It represented an eternal threat to the individual through surrender of agency and self-determination. When compared to unfortunate—but temporary—enslavement during mortality, the enslaving power of sin was much more dangerous. And, just as the enslaving power of sin was central to the concerns of the early Church, it continues to be a primary focus for the Church today. This is demonstrated by modern teachings on the plan of salvation, the need for a body, and the eternal principle of agency.

In addition to being a major doctrine of early Christianity, it was also a topic addressed by Seneca the Younger (3 BC–AD 65). Seneca was a Roman Stoic philosopher, author, and nobleman who served in the court of Nero in Rome. It was a time when religion was completely unconcerned about moral behavior, but rather purposed to placate the gods. Yet in a letter to Lucilis Junior in AD 64, Seneca wrote, "Show me a man who is not a slave; one is a slave to lust, another to greed, another to ambition, and all men are slaves to fear. . . . No servitude is more disgraceful than that which is self-imposed."[175] Even for Seneca, personal surrender of freedom to addiction and avarice was worse than enslavement from consequences beyond a person's control.

It is intriguing to speculate to what degree Seneca's ideas about self-enslavement were influenced by his close associations with Nero, who was a veritable poster child of self-indulgence, hedonism, and enslavement to sin.[176] It is also interesting to wonder to what degree his thoughts could have been molded by Christian teachings that made their way to Rome. There is good evidence that these teachings had penetrated the upper echelons of Roman society. Consider that Paul counted as Saints members of "Caesar's household" in his Epistle to the Philippians.[177] Seneca's other writings provide additional evidence, showing some awareness of the teachings of Jesus Christ.[178]

The writings of Seneca notwithstanding, Paul and Peter[179] made no small impact on the social consciousness of Rome at the time of Nero. Peter decried the bondage that some men bring upon themselves by being slaves of corruption.[180] Paul in particular taught extensively about the enslavement of sin in his Epistle to the Romans.

Romans 6:16–18

Know ye not, that to whom ye yield yourselves servants to obey, his servants ye are to whom ye obey; whether of sin unto death, or of obedience unto righteousness? But God be thanked, that ye were the servants of sin, but ye have obeyed from the heart that form of doctrine which was delivered you. Being then made free from sin, ye became the servants of righteousness.

Once again, the KJV translates *doulos* as "servant" rather than "slave" in a context that Paul is obviously referring to: enslavement by sin. Paul recognized that the "infirmity of [the] flesh"[181] made men vulnerable to becoming "slaves of uncleanness and iniquity."[182] In fact, various Pauline Epistles teach that we become slaves to passions and pleasures,[183] to other gods,[184] to drink,[185] to the law of Moses,[186] to fear of death,[187] to false doctrines,[188] and to the vain deceits and traditions of men.[189]

To the Saints in Rome, Paul recounted his own personal struggle to overcome the infirmity of the flesh. Though trying to live a spiritual law, he knew he was carnal by nature. Paul also referred to this carnal state as being "sold under sin."[190] This is a powerful metaphor that demonstrates how sin enslaves and results in the sale of the sinner to Satan, the master of sin. Paul goes on to humbly admit "for the good that I would I do not: but the evil which I would not, that I do."[191] It is the age-old struggle that ensues as a result of the enslavement of sin. And, because of it, men find themselves in the snare of the devil and "are taken captive by him at his will."[192]

Some of the greatest teachings about the enslavement of sin came from Jesus Christ. The Lord's Prayer speaks directly of our need for forgiveness and deliverance from the enslavement of temptation and evil.[193] In the parable of the prodigal son, the prodigal son confesses his sins and says he should become as the hired slave of his father. But the father's forgiveness saves him from such a fate.[194]

A fair number of Christ's teachings spoke of enslavement to sin in a somewhat metaphorical sense. The Synoptic Gospels describe Christ healing the paralytic and proclaiming that his sins were forgiven.[195] In this case, enslavement of the body to illness and the subsequent healing was like the liberty that comes with the forgiveness of sin. Healing the lepers would've been seen likewise.[196] This disease was considered unclean and resulted in social banishment. It was often thought to be a punishment for sin. Furthermore, such a healing—which Jesus called *cleansing*—would literally bring people back to life because they could rejoin their communities and families, freed from the slavery of their disease. Luke recounts Christ's healing of the "woman with a spirit of infirmity" who couldn't rise up for eighteen years.[197] In healing her, she was not only "loosed" from her illness (like an ox freed from its pen), but also liberated from the bonds of Satan.

Christ taught that conversion with the resulting forgiveness of sins was necessary for unbelievers before they could be freed from being deaf, blind, and unable to understand.[198] Finally, His suffrage of the sin-enslaved woman—wetting his feet with her tears, wiping them with her hair, and then anointing them with ointment—is replete with the metaphor that sin enslaves and repentance frees.[199] The washing of feet was a duty strongly associated with slavery. When Jesus spoke to the sinner and said, "Thy sins are forgiven thee. . . . Thy faith hath saved thee; go in peace," His message offers the hope of forgiveness, freedom, and peace through faithfulness to sinners who demonstrate their love to him.

Jesus Christ's greatest and most direct teachings about the slavery of sin are found in the eighth chapter of John. There were multiple occasions where the teachings of Jesus Christ provoked such outrage among His opponents that they tried to kill Him. But this chapter recounts an event in which some of His disciples abandoned Him and ultimately tried to stone Him.

John 8:31–36

Then said Jesus to those Jews which believed on him, If ye continue in my word, then are ye my disciples indeed; and ye shall know the truth, and the truth shall make you free. They answered him, We be Abraham's seed, and were never in bondage to any man: how sayest thou, Ye shall be made free? Jesus answered them, Verily, verily, I say unto you, Whosoever committeth sin is the servant of sin. And the servant abideth not in the house for ever: but the Son abideth ever. If the Son therefore shall make you free, ye shall be free indeed.

For Jesus to say that the Jews could become free as they learned the truth suggested that they were then enslaved. It has already been noted that it was highly offensive to call someone a slave or suggest that they were slave-like in any way. Herein we see a great double standard. To the free, slavery was okay for others, but an abomination to consider it personally. It seems that they were so outraged at the suggestion that they were in bondage that they stopped listening—and willfully ended their discipleship. It never registered that Jesus was teaching them about a metaphorical bondage to sin that was more devastating than physical bondage. They wouldn't hear the truth and refused to believe it.

To yield to sin was to serve sin, becoming its slave. The Jews took great pride in their Abrahamic lineage and freeborn status.[200] Christ suggested that their tenacious devotion to their sins and unwillingness to abandon them made them into slaves. This enslavement ultimately destroyed their birthright in the Abrahamic family, and it sent them into a rage. When Jesus Christ asserted his status as the great "I am," the lesson was over and He escaped without harm—in spite of their determination to stone Him for blasphemy.

Slavery of sin robs people of their eternal agency. This is as relevant in contemporary society as it was in the days of Jesus and Paul. Sin's capacity to enslave comes in many shapes and forms. Many have been and are enslaved by addictions that so completely take over their wills that they are, in the end, powerless and utterly incapable of defying the addiction.[201] The addictions are endless: alcohol, prescription and illicit drugs, pornography, immorality, social media, Internet, exercise, employment, money, and so on.

In some cases, it is the consequences of sin that have an enslaving effect. This may relate to feelings of guilt, depression, worthlessness, and hopelessness. Scars of sin may manifest later on in relationships, health, financial security, or chances for educational or occupational advancement. The inertia of sin can have an enslaving effect on people so powerful, they never start the repentance process that would free them.

Sinful behavior, in and of itself, can have an enslaving effect on the children of men. Sin becomes a veritable positive feedback loop in which the sin suppresses conscience, loosens the reins that previously restrain it, and allows the unbridled sinner to then press forward at an ever-accelerating pace toward their own destruction. In virtually all cases, sin enslaves by alienating the sinner from the liberating, guiding influence of the Holy Spirit.

Teachings throughout the New Testament affirm that the slavery of sin is the vilest form of slavery. Enslavement of the body to another, as horrific as it was, was temporary. Many slaves could win their freedom; all would ultimately shed its shackles with death. Yet the slavery of sin was of eternal consequence. It robs us of freedom and surrenders our agency to Satan, the master of all who are enslaved to sin. It destroys our possibility of eternal life.

Jesus taught that "no man can serve[202] two masters."[203] If his master is sin, then by definition he cannot simultaneously count Christ as his master as well. The Christian, knowing what he or she knows, should be determined not to serve sin. In reality, any master that displaces God from the primacy of our devotion suffices.[204] The devoted slave of any sin cleaves to his or her master—Satan—essentially choosing to abandon his or her discipleship of Christ. Instead of worshipping God, he or she ends up worshipping sin.

Chapter 6: The Doctrine of Enslavement to Christ

The days surrounding the Crucifixion and death of Jesus Christ were associated with a great deal of confusion and despair for His disciples. It seems that none of the remaining eleven had fully understood the necessity of the literal sacrifice of Jesus Christ to fulfill His mission as Messiah. With the post-Resurrection appearances of Jesus Christ to the Apostles and His forty-day ministry to them, they began to understand His teachings in a new context. Christ's Atonement for men literally made Him *kyrios*—Lord and Master. If Christ was the Master, then they were the slaves. Yet, as Bradley stated, the systematic watering down of the words associated with slavery tends to dilute or even obscure the message.[205]

The figure of the Christian as a slave of Christ or of God is inchoate in a number of Jesus's parables and familiar from the writings of Paul. Christian discourse figuratively plays on moments of reduction to and release from bondage. The twenty-first-century reader can easily lose sight of the context from which these metaphors emerge.[206]

Within days of the Lord's Ascension, Peter began to preach these principles to the people. The day of Pentecost was a Jewish feast day celebrating the harvest, observed fifty days after the Passover. The city of Jerusalem was rather swollen with pilgrims from all across the Jewish Diaspora. As the Saints gathered together on that day, they experienced a miraculous outpouring of the gift of the Holy Ghost. So dramatic was the manifestation that it drew in great crowds of curious onlookers who heard their native language rather than the Galilean dialect of the Christian Saints.

Suddenly the prophecies of Joel[207] had meaning. The promised outpouring of the Spirit of the Lord on all flesh had been realized. The recipient of this gift was "my servants and . . . my handmaidens."[208] These "servants" and "handmaidens" were respectively *doulos* and *doule*: God's male and female slaves. The concept of men being slaves of God would not have been foreign to the Jews who listened. Similarly, the idea that they had to "call on the name of the Lord [to] be saved"[209] would also have been familiar. But the notion that "God hath made that same Jesus, whom ye have crucified, both Lord and Christ"[210] was earth-shattering. Jesus of Nazareth was the Master, and it was only His name that had power to save.

The day of Pentecost was a watershed moment that changed the way men viewed their relationship with God. Heretofore, the Jews were slaves of God, who had redeemed them *collectively* from Egypt or Babylon. Now men and women were slaves of Christ, who had redeemed them *individually* through His atoning sacrifice. Henceforth, it would be less about obedience to God as a people and more about devotion to Christ individually.

Almost immediately, the Biblical record explodes with references to this new relationship: the Christian as slave and Christ as master. Peter began referring to himself as "a [slave][211] and an apostle of Jesus Christ." Jude referred to himself as "the [slave][212] of Jesus Christ, and brother of James." John the Revelator not only referred to himself as a slave of the God, but also the Saints and their leaders as slaves of God.[213] Paul, in teaching Timothy of how to be an effective leader, referred to him as "the [slave][214] of the Lord." He also makes reference to the Apostles using words that convey the unmistakable imagery of slavery.[215] Luke referred to Paul, Silas, and himself as "[slaves][216] of the most high God." Additionally, there are several references in the New Testament that use the term *syndoulos,* or "fellowslave." This includes a number of self-references in John's Revelation,[217] as well as Pauline references to fellow missionaries Epahras and Tychius.[218] Numerous other examples could be cited.[219]

These multiple references allude to the importance of "the Christian as slave and Christ as master" relationship. Paul was undoubtedly the one who solidified and further developed the doctrine into something that was foundational how early Church members saw their relationship with Jesus Christ.

Paul repeatedly referred to himself as a slave of Jesus Christ.[220] He also referred to his labors in behalf of the Lord as those rendered by a slave.[221] Paul speaks of his body bearing "the marks of the Lord Jesus Christ,"[222] yet another reference to Paul's personal enslavement to Christ. The word translated in the KJV as "marks" stems from the Greek word *stigma*. Thayer's Lexicon defines stigma as "a mark pricked in or branded upon the body. To ancient oriental usage, slaves and soldiers bore the name or the stamp of their master or commander branded or pricked (cut) into their bodies to indicate what master or general they belonged to, and there were even some devotee's who stamped themselves in this way with the token of their gods."[223]

Paul's body bore the marks of his many years of service to God: persecutions,[224] stoning,[225] beatings, shipwreck,[226] imprisonment,[227] arraignments,[228] and decades as an itinerant minister of the gospel. In Galatians, he uses wordplay, with the scars being likened to the brands placed on slaves to indicate their owner. And, in so doing, illustrates the need for enslavement to Christ as a marker of total conversion.

So complete was Paul's vision of himself as Christ's humble slave that it created a few public relations issues with some of the Corinthian Saints. Paul consistently rejected the financial support of the churches where he ministered.[229] Instead, it was his habit to support himself by plying his trade as a tentmaker,[230] thereby teaching the Saints principles of industry and self-reliance.[231]

For a high-ranking official of the Church to willingly perform manual labor was highly unusual in a society dominated by patronage of the noble class. Paul's industry made himself appear servile in the eyes of the Greeks and Roman elite—quite the opposite of what they considered attributes of a wise man or a true philosopher.[232] Martin pointed out that such attitudes were shaped by Greek philosophy. Socrates considered manual labor to be abhorrent and degrading. This view was adopted and perpetuated by his student Plato and Aristotle, who followed him.[233] As a result, it became the prevailing view of Greek and Latin elite for centuries[234] and was certainly the sentiment of some of the Corinthian Saints. It seems that some held the view that manual labor was shameful, humiliating, and out of keeping with a leader of the Church.[235]

Paul addressed these concerns by reiterating the contention that he was the slave of Christ and laboring as His slave was not demeaning. He takes this further by arguing that he was a slave of special status: a slave steward, so a leader of the Christian Church.

> Paul sets up a rhetorical trap for these opponents. He admits to working under compulsion: he serves involuntarily, like a slave, and for that reason deserves no wage. His more educated opponents nod vigorously. "Ah, so you are a slave after all, as we have implied?" "Yes," answers Paul, "a slave of *Christ*. In fact, Christ's slave *steward*." Immediately, Paul has defused their criticism and accusation. . . . Once Paul defines himself as a slave in this sense, no one within the Christian community can criticize his self-characterization. Furthermore, within the common Christian discourse, Paul's slavery to Christ has a positive connotation—as a high-status designation—especially for lower-class people.[236]

Paul depicted himself as slave of higher status. Martin called him a *slave steward* in 1 Corinthians 9:16–18, reminiscent of slave stewards in the parable of the talents. Verse 17 refers to Paul's dispensation (Greek *oikonomeo*,[237] meaning to be a steward or to manage household affairs).[238] Though a slave of Christ, as Christ's steward over the Church, Paul had authority and stature among the rest of the slaves of the household. His legitimacy as a leader of the Christians was thereby maintained.

Given Paul's background and training in the arts of philosophy and rhetoric, his attitude speaks volumes of his humility and devotion to the work of Christ. Here we see the application of Paul's assertion that he was not ashamed of the gospel of Christ[239] and tangible proof that his concept of enslavement to Him was not merely metaphorical.

The teachings of Peter on the day of Pentecost demonstrate that the idea of enslavement to Christ was not one of Paul's creations.[240] Yet, Paul's conception of enslavement to Christ was almost certainly colored by his history of persecution, arraignment, and imprisonment for the cause on so many occasions. Paul was arrested on his return to Jerusalem in AD 57 and was taken into custody when he caused a tumult at the temple. He was transferred to Caesarea and held for two years before exercising his rights as a Roman citizen to appeal before Emperor Nero. While enroute to Rome, he was shipwrecked in Malta.

He later arrived in Rome in AD 60 and spent two years under house arrest. It is estimated that Paul spent five to six years of his life in prison. Tradition holds that he was beheaded[241] in around AD 65 in Rome under the order of Nero.

In his captivity Epistles,[242] Paul frequently referred to himself as a prisoner of Jesus Christ.[243] These Epistles capture Paul's tribulation and suffering with such poignancy that we are drawn in to the prison with him.[244] He spoke of his love and concern for the Saints while in prison,[245] begging them to remember him and his message.[246] Though Paul lost everything for the gospel,[247] he rejoiced in his opportunity to suffer for the cause of Christ.[248] While replete with references to his personal suffering,[249] Paul's letters overwhelmingly speak of strength, determination, and confidence[250] in the Lord's support in overcoming adversity.[251]

As complete as Paul's view of himself was as the Lord's slave, he also realized the necessity of "the Christian as slave and Christ as master" relationship for all members of the Church. Even as Paul describes "the slaves of Chloe"[252] as belonging to her, he frequently describes to the Saints as "belonging to Christ."[253] Just as a slave's only purpose is to do the will of the master, Paul's life was one of continuous submission to the will of God and ceaseless efforts to please Him. Likewise, Paul saw the Christian's duty, as the slave of Christ, as putting God's will before his or her own, and "[do] the will of God from the heart."[254]

Chapter 7: Christ's Ransom of the Captive Soul

Epictetus was a Stoic philosopher in the middle of the first century AD. He was born a slave in Hieropoplis, Phyrgia (today Pamukkale, Turkey), and owned by Epaphroditus,[255] a wealthy freedman who served as a secretary to Nero in Rome. He was known to be lame—one source alleges that his master deliberately fractured his leg in a fit of anger.[256] Later in life, Epictetus was able to gain his freedom. Following his manumission, he developed his philosophical theories and advanced them by starting his own school.

His philosophical thought seemed largely preoccupied with freedom, liberty, and self-control.[257] With time, he developed a theory that true freedom comes through freedom of spirit and mind—not freedom of the physical body. It's not surprising that such meditations would come from someone whose early life was so devoid of liberty. For most of his life, he was denied these things *because he was a slave*. He longed for freedom of self-determination, yet was perpetually subjected to the desires of his master. He longed for the ability to control his own body, but he had no power to protect it from the vengeful rage of his owner. As a result, he was forced to live out his days as a cripple. According to Epictetus, the longing for liberty and freedom is a constant obsession for a slave.[258] He described slaves as perpetually praying for freedom, but they often lived out their days with their prayers unrealized. His perspective, more than any other ancient writer, emphasized the utterly hopeless condition of the slave.

Titus Maccius Plautus (254–184 BC), the great Roman playwright, portrayed another slave perspective. In his comedy *Amphitryon*, Plautus captured the scornful mutterings of the slave Sosia as he was out in a dangerous neighborhood on a midnight errand:

> A rich man's servant leads a lousy life.
> All his nights and days it's just a constant strife,
> To keep up with the errands and jobs he has to do,
> With never a moments peace or rest for you.
> What wealthy master's done work himself? Not one!
> So what ever a man can think up, he thinks can be done.
> So a slave runs into wrongs of every kind.
> You have to sweat—and shrug and be resigned.[259]

It was not just the ceaseless work, but also the realization that one was a slave and nothing could change that. It was an ever-present fear of punishment, an unending weariness of both body and mind, and the unrelenting knowledge that tomorrow would be more of the same.

A third perspective lies in Paul's view. In this instance, he spoke not as a slave of men, but rather as a slave of sin. Paul knew the enslaving power of sin. Though taught by all the prophets, none of them stated the universal enslavement of man to sin more succinctly than Paul: "For all have sinned, and come short of the glory of God."[260] This caused Paul to express the sense of despair that grips the hearts of all those who perceive their enslavement to sin: "O wretched man that I am! who shall deliver me from the body of this death?"[261]

The Slave's Need for Ransom

Both slave and sinner are in the hopeless position, being powerless to end their misery. They are both totally dependent on forces beyond their control to bring about their freedom. For the slave, it is the freedom of emancipation. For the sinner, it is the freedom of forgiveness. For the latter, it requires more than the forgiveness of man; it necessitates the forgiveness of God. In both cases, they need redemption. Just as ransom is the hope of the slave, Christ is the hope of the sinner.[262]

No teaching of the New Testament is more prominent than the redemptive power of Jesus Christ's Atonement, death, and Resurrection in ending the enslavement of sin. It is the essence of the good news of Christ's gospel. Yet without understanding the slavery metaphor, our understanding of Christ as our Redeemer is impaired.

As with all essential elements of Christ's gospel, this teaching found its origins in the teachings of the prophets before Christ's mission even began.[263] Consider the prophecy of the angel who reassured Joseph and instructed him to take Mary as his wife:

Matthew 1:20–21 (emphasis added)

The angel of the Lord appeared unto him in a dream, saying, Joseph, thou son of David, fear not to take unto thee Mary thy wife: for that which is conceived in her is of the Holy Ghost. And she shall bring forth a son, and thou shalt call his name Jesus: *for he shall save his people from their sins.*

Matthew's account is unique as the Lord saves us from our sins—not from destruction on the battlefield or captivity. In summarizing His mission to His Apostles, Jesus said,

Matthew 20:26–28[264] (emphasis added)

Whosoever will be great among you, let him be your minister; and whosoever will be chief among you, let him be your servant: even as the Son of man came not to be ministered unto, but to minister, and to give his life a *ransom* for many.

This passage of scripture teaches two great truths that need further commentary. First, Christ came as a slave. Second, His life would serve as a ransom for many.

Christ Came as a Slave

The prophet Isaiah frequently spoke of the long-awaited Messiah as coming in the role of a slave.[265] Matthew quoted Isaiah's reference to Christ when he said, "Behold my [slave], whom I have chosen; my beloved, in whom my soul is well pleased."[266] The Savior Himself said He came to minister (*diakoneō*[267])—to be a slave.[268] In all things, He led by example.[269] The examples of His role as a servant, a minister and a slave are beyond the scope of this work to cite in a comprehensive way. However, a fitting example of Jesus Christ's role as a slave is found in John's account of Jesus washing the feet of the Twelve.[270]

John 13:4–5

He riseth from supper, and laid aside his garments; and took a towel, and girded himself. After that he poureth water into a basin, and began to wash the disciples' feet, and to wipe them with the towel wherewith he was girded.

For most people, the expression *to gird yourself* is metaphorical and emphasizes our need to prepare the mind and body for the work of the Lord.[271] But the practical aspects of the phrase—which related to clothing styles of the era—may be lost to us today. In ancient times, the common dress of the day was a cotton or linen tunic. The tunic was worn over a loincloth with possibly an inner tunic (or undergarment) for the upper body, depending on how cold it was. For women, the tunics were ankle length. For men, they extended to the knee in the Greco-Roman[272] world but may well have been ankle length in the Levant.[273] The tunic was secured with a girdle around the waist. The girdle was made of colorful wool or silk for women and sometimes extended down toward the knees like an apron. A man's girdle was a leather belt that could be used to carry things. When heavier articles were carried, shoulder straps could be added to the girdle. A cloak or mantle was worn over the tunic.

The clothing of slaves matched their work.[274] Some had nothing to wear or just wore loincloths or threadbare tunics. Domestic and farm slaves often wore a short tunic, shepherds had a sleeveless tunic with the right shoulder bare, and fishermen wore only a loincloth.[275]

For slave and freeborn alike, a long tunic could get in the way or cause stumbling when working or moving quickly. If a man needed to work, run, or fight,[276] he would prepare himself by tucking the hem of his tunic into the girdle around his waist. The process was known as *girding the loins*, or simply girding.

John's account of Christ washing the feet of the Twelve is highly charged with images of slavery. Prior to washing the feet of the Twelve, Jesus removed His cloak and thus was clothed like a slave. John describes Christ girding Himself, reminiscent of the slaves who serve the master in the parable of the unprofitable servants.[277] It is also reminiscent of Luke's references to the parable of the ten virgins and the unexpected service of the faithful slaves by the master of the house.[278]

The act of washing the feet was strongly associated with the duties of a slave. It was considered beneath the dignity of a Jewish slave to wash feet.[279] It is therefore not surprising that Peter objects to his Lord performing such a servile task by saying, "Thou shalt never wash my feet."[280] Though he did not understand the ordinance,[281] he willingly accepted it and trusted the Lord who taught that even the Messiah was expected to assume the role of a slave for the work of God.

John 13:12–16

So after he had washed their feet, and had taken his garments, and was set down again, he said unto them, Know ye what I have done to you? Ye call me Master and Lord: and ye say well; for so I am. If I then, your Lord and Master, have washed your feet; ye also ought to wash one another's feet. For I have given you an example, that ye should do as I have done to you. Verily, verily, I say unto you, The servant is not greater than his lord; neither he that is sent greater than he that sent him.

Some of His final mortal teachings focused on teaching the Twelve humility, service, and the unquestioning obedience that is expected of a faithful slave. Not only were His final actions demonstrative of His role as slave to His Father's will,[282] but so was the way He died. In the end, He was betrayed for thirty silver shekels,[283] or the price of a slave,[284] and died in the manner by which the Romans executed a slave: He was tortured by scourging and crucified.

In the second chapter of Philippians, Paul taught that Jesus "made himself of no reputation, and took upon him the form of a [slave]"[285] and humbled Himself to death by crucifixion.

> Death on the cross was the penalty for slaves, as everyone knew; as such it symbolized extreme humiliation, shame and torture. . . . The one who had died the death of a slave was exalted to be Lord of the whole creation and bearer of the divine name *Kyrios*.[286]

Early Christian teachings in the Greco-Roman world were met with a great deal of skepticism. Paul cited that the notion of a crucified God of the Christian faith was considered foolishness to the Greeks and was a great stumblingblock to the Jews.[287] Crucifixion was considered such a shameful death that many had a hard time taking Christianity seriously because of the way that Jesus died. And yet Paul's teachings to the Romans went beyond Christ being crucified and resurrected. He used the image of crucifixion to demonstrate that our sins are killed through Christ's Atonement while we are raised in a newness of life, free from sin's enslavement.

Romans 6:6–7

Knowing this, that our old man is crucified with him, that the body of sin might be destroyed, that henceforth we should not serve sin. For he that is dead is freed from sin.

With this imagery, Paul taught that crucifixion—a form of death usually reserved for the slaves and vile criminals—was an allegory for the death of the sinner. Similarly, Christ's Resurrection was analogous to our rebirth as we are liberated from the bondage and enslavement of sin. Christ's Crucifixion and Atonement made it possible for us to be redeemed by another master: even Jesus Christ. The old man, laden with sin and addiction and a shameful past, has his sins and old self crucified, a fitting death for a slave. As the slave of sin is destroyed, the slave of Christ is born.

Galatians 2:20

I am crucified with Christ: nevertheless I live; yet not I, but Christ liveth in me: and the life which I now live in the flesh I live by the faith of the Son of God, who loved me, and gave himself for me.

Christ as the Ransom for Many

On top of depicting Christ as the faithful slave of God, Matthew 20:28 promises that He would "give his life a ransom for many." The many ways that the Savior fulfilled the demands of the law of sacrifice outlined in the law of Moses are also beyond the scope of this work.[288] Suffice it to say that He was the Lamb of God: the firstborn male, sinless and without blemish. His blood alone could provide ransom for the collective sins of man. As Paul stated, "Christ our Passover is sacrificed for us."[289]

The Greek word for ransom is λύτρον—*lytron.*[290] Thayer's lexicon[291] defines *lytron* as the price for redeeming or ransom of slaves, captives, or a person's life. From a theological perspective, it refers to the price paid to liberate the repentant from the misery and enslavement of their sins. Though this passage in Matthew 20 (and the parallel passage in Mark 10) is the only use of *lytron* in the New Testament, the concept is universally taught throughout the scriptures. Paul used the related term λυτρόω—*lytroo*[292]—to teach Titus how we are purified and redeemed from sin:

Titus 2:13–14 (emphasis added)

Looking for that blessed hope, and the glorious appearing of the great God and our Saviour Jesus Christ; who gave himself for us, that he might *redeem* us from all iniquity, and purify unto himself a peculiar people, zealous of good works.

Peter used the same word to teach that the redemptive price paid to liberate us from the slavery of sin was not made in silver or gold currency. Rather, it was paid "with the precious blood of Christ, as of a lamb without blemish and without spot."[293] The author of Hebrews uses a second related word (λύτρωσις—*lytrōsis*)[294] to describe how Christ's blood brings eternal redemption to us.[295] Finally, Paul uses a third derivative (ἀντίλυτρον—*antilytron*)[296] in order to teach Timothy about redemption:

1 Timothy 2:5–6 (emphasis added)

For there is one God, and one mediator between God and men, the man Christ Jesus; who gave himself a *ransom* for all, to be testified in due time.

Thayer's lexicon defines *antilytron* as "that which is given in exchange for another as the price of his redemption."[297] Christ's Atonement is the thing—the ransom paid—that loosens the bonds of slavery of sin; His Resurrection is the miracle that saves us from everlasting death.

The Lord's Purchased Possessions

The first fourteen verses of Paul's Epistle to the Ephesians exemplify how Paul saw the ransomed Saints: as the Lord's personal possessions. Paul relates how the Saints were chosen[298] and foreordained.[299] Their sins were forgiven as they were redeemed through the blood of Christ.[300] The Holy Spirit sealed them after they believed the good news of the gospel. Christ's redemption was the earnest money and the Saints the *purchased possession*.[301]

Paul's depiction of the Saints as the Lord's *purchased possessions* is in keeping with the concept of persons as property—as slaves. New Testament translators have used the word *peripoiēsis*, which means "a possession or one's own property," in a variety of ways. It is translated as the "purchased possession" in Ephesians 1:14 of the KJV. It is also rendered as "obtain" elsewhere in the New Testament. For example, Paul promised the Saints of Thessalonica that they would obtain the glory of the Lord Jesus Christ. In this case, just as he pointed out to the Ephesians, they were chosen and sanctified by the Spirit by their belief of the gospel of the Savior.[302] Paul also used *peripoiēsis* to describe salvation as personal property *obtained* by those who are redeemed by Jesus Christ, the Master.

1 Thessalonians 5:9–10

For God hath not appointed us to wrath, but to obtain salvation by our Lord Jesus Christ, who died for us, that, whether we wake or sleep, we should live together with him.

Finally, the author of Hebrews uses *peripoiēsis* in describing how the just will prevail by saving—or gaining possession—of their souls from perdition.[303]

Peter also speaks of the Lord's people as having been purchased or owned. He too makes use of this unique word. In this instance, *peripoiēsis* is translated as "peculiar." He calls the Saints "a chosen generation, a royal priesthood, an holy nation, a peculiar people" (1 Peter 2:9). A large part of what dignifies the Saints is that they belong to the Lord, having been chosen (elected or hand-picked).[304] The slave does not choose his master, but rather the master chooses his slave.

Paul uses similar verbiage in his Epistle to Titus. In this case, he uses the related word *periousios,* which also means "one's possession."[305]

Titus 2:13–14

Looking for that blessed hope, and the glorious appearing of the great God and our Saviour Jesus Christ; who gave himself for us, that he might redeem us from all iniquity, and purify unto himself a peculiar people, zealous of good works.

There was a logical extension from the enslaved sinner becoming the property of his new master after being redeemed. This concept, taught by Peter, Paul, and the author of Hebrews, is closely tied to the idea of being chosen of the Lord. It was the Lord who chose His people, and it was the Lord who redeemed them.

Bought with a Price

Peter's second epistle to the early Church captures his outrage upon hearing of false prophets who denied the redemptive nature and power of Christ's Atonement.

2 Peter 2:1 (emphasis added)

But there were false prophets also among the people, even as there shall be false teachers among you, who privily shall bring in damnable heresies, even denying the Lord that *bought* them, and bring upon themselves swift destruction.

While stamping out such heresies, Peter also emphasized the reality of a ransom being paid for us. This ransom liberates us from the chains of sin as we stand helpless in the slave market.[306] It is the Lord who bought us.

Paul taught similar concepts. In his farewell to the Ephesian Saints, Paul charged them to "feed the church of God, which [Christ] hath purchased with his own blood."[307] He taught the Corinthians that their bodies were temples of the Holy Ghost—not their own—bought with the price of Christ's Atonement. Quite literally, God owned them, both body and soul.[308] The idea that "good money" had been used to purchase us from the slavery of sin was a powerful symbol for these early Saints, and one that Paul used often in his teachings. Consider how regularly Paul taught these principles to congregations of the Church throughout the Mediterranean world:

1 Corinthians 7:23 (emphasis added)

Ye are *bought* with a price; be not ye the servants of men.

Romans 8:2

For the law of the Spirit of life in Christ Jesus hath made me free from the law of sin and death.

Galatians 4:3–5 (emphasis added)

Even so we, when we were children, were in bondage under the elements of the world: but when the fulness of the time was come, God sent forth his Son, made of a woman, made under the law, to *redeem* them that were under the law.

Colossians 1:13–14 (emphasis added)

[God] hath delivered us from the power of darkness, and hath translated us into the kingdom of his dear Son: in whom we have *redemption* through his blood, even the forgiveness of sins.

Romans 5:8–11

But God commendeth his love toward us, in that, while we were yet sinners, Christ died for us. Much more then, being now justified by his blood, we shall be saved from wrath through him. For if, when we were enemies, we were reconciled to God by the death of his Son, much more, being reconciled, we shall be saved by his life. And not only so, but we also joy in God through our Lord Jesus Christ, by whom we have now received the atonement.

Other examples are so numerous that it belabors the point to cite them all. Paul consistently gloried in the redemptive power of Christ's Atonement in liberating us from the captivity of sin. And in the process, he regularly referred to the *freedom* associated with our ransom from sin. Though many of Paul's writings are closely associated with themes of slavery and captivity on both a personal level[309] and a metaphorical level,[310] it is the promise of freedom through Christ's Atonement that is the driving force behind his use of slavery metaphors.

Freedom through Enslavement

In his statistical analysis of Greek words associated with *freedom*, Murray Harris found that Paul champions the idea that people are made free through Christ's ransom more than any other New Testament author.[311] He argues from his data (summarized below) that Paul can be more aptly thought of as "the Apostle of freedom."

Greek Word	Translation	Uses by Paul	Uses in the NT
Eleutheria (noun)	Freedom	7[312]	11
Apeleutheros (noun)	Freed person	1[313]	1
Eleutheros (adjective)	Free	16[314]	23
Eleutheroō (verb)	Set free	5[315]	7

Though all Paul's Epistles teach of the liberty that comes from the Atonement, his Epistle to the Galatians is the most comprehensive and has been called Paul's "charter of freedom."[316] He compares slavery and freedom respectively to Ishmael (born of Sarah's slave, Hagar) and Isaac (born of Abraham's freeborn wife, Sarah).[317] Paul reassures us that "we are not children of the bondwoman,[318] but of the free."[319] As a result, we are "no more a servant, but a son; and if a son, then an heir of God through Christ."[320] With this knowledge and the reassurance it brings, we are better able to resist the forces of sin that threaten "the liberty we have in Christ Jesus."[321] We are then better able to rise to Paul's great challenge:

Galatians 5:1

Stand fast therefore in the liberty wherewith Christ hath made us free, and be not entangled again with the yoke of bondage.

But was our freedom really so sweet if it merely meant a different master to whom we would have to subject ourselves? We must not forget that the ransom from sin simultaneously enslaved the sinner to Christ. Murray Harris[322] referred to this concept as the Christian paradox: *freedom leads to slavery and slavery leads to freedom*. In Harris's words, "Freedom from slavery is followed by freedom in slavery."[323] Similarly, Michael Card points out that "[Jesus] came in the form of a slave, not to offer us freedom from slavery but a new kind of slavery that is freedom."[324]

Harris also illustrated a second paradox of first-century Christian thought. At this time, philosophers such as Euripides and Seneca were developing a concept known as the Stoic Paradox: "a slave in body, yet free in spirit." In contrast, every Christian, whether slave or free, was spiritually free yet a slave to Christ: "free, yet a slave."[325]

This reality of simultaneous liberation and enslavement is perhaps one of the greatest forgotten paradoxes in scripture.

> Many of the Bible's most provocative truths appear to us as paradoxical. Consider, for example, the truth that salvation is both free and costly, that to be truly rich you must be poor in spirit, or that to find your life you must lose it, or that to be wise you must embrace the foolishness of the gospel. Scripture teaches us that those who mourn will be comforted; those who give will receive; those who are least will be greatest; those who are humbled will be exalted; those who are last will be first.[326]

Just as great truths of the gospel are sometimes conveyed through the use of paradox, so it is with the Christian Paradox. The paradox of freedom through enslavement to Christ is multifaceted. This liberty can be realized through freedom from our former master (sin) by liberation through the name of our new master, and by freedom through the promise of adoption. The ultimate freedom is realized as we surrender to the Master the only thing that is truly ours: our will.

Chapter 8: Jesus Christ—A New Master

The experiences of a slave, more than anything else, was dependent on the nature of his master. Prior to ransom by Christ, the sinner was subjected to the worst of masters: Satan. Satan is the master of sin. In scripture, the word most consistently used to describe Satan is *miserable*.[327] Having fallen from heaven, he "[became] miserable forever, and sought also the misery of all mankind."[328] "He seeketh all men to be miserable like unto himself."[329]

His miserable nature was reflected in the plight of his slaves. The scriptures often associate Satan with weeping, wailing, and gnashing of teeth.[330] Peter likened the devil's slaves to "servants of corruption" and "brute beasts" that "cannot cease from sin."[331] Remember, Simon (the sorcerer of Samaria) who, though baptized by Philip, clung to his first master. Of him, Peter said, "I perceive that thou art in the gall of bitterness, and in the bond of iniquity."[332] It's no fun being enslaved to sin.

As slaves of Satan, we labor under the worst of masters. Our state is not only miserable, but also hopeless. The master of sin promises people pseudo-freedom that enslaves more completely. It is manifested in a thousand different ways: overpowering addiction, obstinate pride, the unquenchable appetite of self-indulgence, and more. He cares not for us and makes no effort to attend to our welfare or needs.[333]

From this miserable existence being enslaved by sin, we are invited to serve a new master.

Matthew 11:28–30 (emphasis added)

Come unto me, all ye that labour and are heavy laden, and *I will give you rest.* Take my yoke upon you, and learn of me; for I am meek and lowly in heart: and ye shall find rest unto your souls. For *my yoke is easy, and my burden is light.*

So in contrast to Satan's promise of pseudo-freedom that enslaves us, Christ promises us pseudo-slavery that frees. Where Satan is the thief and hireling, Christ is the good shepherd. Not only does He love the sheep, but also gives His life for them. Where Satan is cruel, Christ is kind and loving. We are promised that because of our good master, we will be anxious for nothing[334] and that all things will work for our good if we love Him.[335] Not only does He forgive us, He forgets our sins.[336] With Him as our master, we will be fearless before men, knowing He will never leave us or forsake us.[337] The knowledge that nothing can separate us from His love[338] brings a peace to our minds that surpasses all understanding.[339]

Freed from the slavery of sin, we become slaves of righteousness and ultimately holiness.[340] It is no small irony that while enjoying Christ's ransom from the enslavement of sin, man is simultaneous enslaved to Christ. Yet, in spite of this, the New Testament message (and especially Paul's message) remains thoroughly optimistic. Our new enslavement represents the only sure road to freedom. This optimism and confidence rested solely on the good nature of Christ.

Romans 6:16–18 (emphasis added)

Know ye not, that to whom ye yield yourselves servants to obey, his servants ye are to whom ye obey; whether of sin unto death, or of obedience unto righteousness? But God be thanked, that ye were the servants of sin, but ye have obeyed from the heart that form of doctrine which was delivered you. *Being then made free from sin, ye became the servants of righteousness.*

The goal of a slave is simple: to obey and please his master. When the master is kind and loving, the yoke becomes easy and the burden light.[341] It therefore becomes easier for us to yield our hearts to him and acknowledge him as our master.

When we call Jesus "Lord," we are acknowledging Him as our sole Master. The Greek word for Lord is *kyrios*, and it occurs nearly 750 times in the New Testament. Its fundamental meaning is "master" or "owner," making it the rational counterpart to the slave (*doulos*). *Kyrios* and *doulos* are two sides of the same relationship. To be a *doulos* was to have a master. Vice versa, a *kyrios* by definition was the owner of slaves. To call Christ the "Lord" is to simultaneously identify Him as Master and ourselves as His slaves.[342]

I Have Chosen You

Discipleship of Christ is a conscious decision. We choose to believe, to commit, and to obey. This is a critical element of lasting discipleship and an essential attribute of disciples who hope to endure to the end. But an equally important concept is that Christ's slaves are chosen by Him. Jesus told the Twelve:

John 15:16

> Ye have not chosen me, but I have chosen you.

This was another paradox that served to reinforce the master-slave relationship that heavily colored the interactions of the Last Supper. Seated around Jesus were twelve men who had sacrificed everything to be with Him. They had left their families, their professions, and their nets, all so they could follow the carpenter who had repaired their boats. They had been with Him through thick and thin, at the height of His popularity as well as in the darker moments when His difficult doctrines had driven many of His "disciples" away.[343] They protected Him from the thronging crowds and stood by Him in the midst of plotting conspirators. Yet now, He thought it important to ignore all this and remind them that He had chosen them.

The Jews generally chose their teacher and then decided to become disciples.[344] So it was for most of the Twelve. They, in their search for truth, had sought Him out and chosen to become disciples. Some were followers of John the Baptist, but all had been looking for the Messias.[345] But consider the fact that the slave doesn't choose the master, but rather the master chooses the slave. Jesus found it necessary to emphasize to the Twelve Apostles that He had chosen them.

Our tendency to soften the negative stigma associated with such a sacred event by viewing the Twelve as *servants*, not *slaves*, distorts the scriptural record and dilutes the meaning of the message. The theme of enslavement to Christ punctuates the entire Last Supper. Jesus was the master; the Twelve were His hand-selected slaves. He had a great work for them to do. Servants are hired and could choose whether or not to work. A slave is owned with no choice in the matter. The master chooses him; he does not choose the master.[346]

Surely their minds took them back to Christ teaching the parable of the talents.[347] Jesus would be leaving "into a far country to receive for himself a kingdom, and to return."[348] He now called together His slaves so He could give them each of them their stewardship. Just as the master expected his slaves to improve on the talents he gave them, so too did Christ expected the Apostles to bring forth fruit and be productive slaves.[349]

The notion that he had been chosen of Jesus Christ is pervasive in the writings of Paul. He speaks of himself as a prisoner, a captive, and a slave of Christ. On the road to Tarsus, it wasn't Saul who chose Christ. He was chosen and forever enslaved. He spoke of being "apprehended of Christ Jesus" and bereft of all possessions because of this enslavement. Yet Paul counted such possessions worthless compared to his ransom by the Savior.

Philippians 3:8–12 (English Standard Version)

Indeed, I count everything as loss because of the surpassing worth of knowing Christ Jesus my Lord. For his sake I have suffered the loss of all things and count them as rubbish, in order that I may gain Christ and be found in him, not having a righteousness of my own that comes from the law, but that which comes through faith in Christ, the righteousness from God that depends on faith—that I may know him and the power of his resurrection, and may share his sufferings, becoming like him in his death, that by any means possible I may attain the resurrection from the dead. Not that I have already obtained this or am already perfect, but I press on to make it my own, because Christ Jesus has made me his own.[350]

Though called and dramatically enslaved to the Master, Paul taught that this calling wasn't limited to the Apostles of the Lord. The calling is extended to all of Christ's slaves. He frequently referred to the Saints as having been "called to be saints."[351] As the Saints came to identify themselves as slaves of Jesus Christ, it became practice to call themselves by the name of their master.

The Name of Christ

Some scholars suggest that just as *Caesarian* means "slave of Caesar," so *Christian* means "slave of Christ."[352] There is little doubt that, in ancient times, the identity of the slave was wrapped up in the name of his or her master. In speaking of "those of the house of Chloe" and the "household of Stephanas,"[353] Paul was referring to the slaves of Chloe and Stephanas, much as he referred to the Saints as the slaves of Christ.[354]

Aristotle taught that a slave is a sharer of the life of the owner. The more noble and glorious the master, the greater the honor and prestige of his slave. This was true of slavery in the Roman Empire to an even greater degree than it was in ancient Greece. Enslavement to Caesar or a member of the senatorial class was a mechanism of social mobility. For a peasant living in poverty, voluntary enslavement to a noble, followed by manumission, could open the doors of opportunity. As his master's freedman, his earning potential and status in the community would be far greater than lifelong freedom as an impoverished commoner.[355] Similarly, from a theological perspective, changing masters from Satan to Christ was an unsurpassable improvement.[356] This principle had great appeal to the mind of the Christian convert at this time in history, as evidenced by the writings of Philo.

> The purified mind rejoices in nothing more than in confessing that it has for its master the One who is Lord of all. For to be the slave of God is the greatest human boast, and is a more precious treasure not only than freedom but even than wealth or dominion or any that mortals cherish.[357]

Yet for the truly converted Christian, it was (and is) about far more than having a master with an esteemed name. It was in Antioch that the followers of Christ first became identified by the name *Christians*.[358] Ignatius was one of the early Church leaders in Antioch. Legend holds that because of his refusal to bow down to the cult deities of Rome, he was arrested and taken before Emperor Trajan, who was wintering in Antioch. Before Trajan, he boldly testified of Christ and was therefore sentenced to die. He was placed in chains, taken all the way to Rome, and literally thrown to the lions in the Colosseum. For Ignatius, it was not enough to simply be *called* a Christian, but rather he had to *be* a Christian with his actions.

> Only pray for me, that God would give me both inward and outward strength so that I may not only be called a Christian, but be discovered to be one. For if I shall demonstrate myself to be a Christian, I may then deservedly be called one, and be thought faithful when I shall no longer appear to the world.[359]

John MacArthur cited a number of additional examples in which early converts to Christianity were so completely identified with the name of Christ that they refused to be known by any other name.[360] They were willing to die horrific deaths and withstand privation and torture of every kind while remaining steadfast in their devotion to the name of Jesus Christ.

Eusebius recounted the story of Sanctus, a Christian from Gaul who was arrested when, under the rule of Marcus Aurelius, it was illegal to be Christian. Despite being subjected to torture over many days, Sanctus refused to divulge his name, his city, or his nation when questioned by persecutors. Instead, he would only reply "I am a Christian." Frustrated by his determination and strength of conviction, he was taken to the amphitheater, forced to run the gauntlet, ravaged by wild beasts, and then roasted alive on an iron chair.[361]

Northcote provided evidence from epitaphs of the catacombs that showed this type of thinking among the early Christian community was common. Speaking of Christians that were being questioned by the authorities, he said,

> They [replied] to all questionings about them the short but comprehensive answer, "I am a Christian." Again and again they caused no little perplexity to their judges by the pertinacity with which they adhered to this brief profession of faith. The question was repeated, "Who are you?" and they replied, "I have already said that I am a Christian; and he who says that has thereby named his country, his family, his profession, and all things else besides." [Others would reply]: "I am a slave of Caesar," they said, "but a Christian who has received his liberty from Christ Himself"; or, contrariwise, "I am a free man, the slave of Christ."[362]

We can begin to understand the centrality of the "name of Christ" in defining what it means to be His disciple. It remains as true for us today as it did for the Saints in the early Church. At that time, to write your name on something, in the Hebrew tradition, was to make it completely your own.[363] Therefore, to be Christ's, we must have His name. This could explain the wording of "taking on the name of Christ" through baptism.

Harris described how early converts were baptized *into the name of Jesus Christ.*[364] He said, "In commercial usage, this Greek phrase *eis to onoma* [into the name] denoted transference of ownership, as in when money is paid 'in the name of' someone."[365] Therefore, baptism into the name of Jesus transfers ownership to Him, who has ransomed us from sin. Disciples of Christ submit to baptism and take on the name of Christ to demonstrate love, devotion, and commitment to serve Him forever.

The members of the early Church lived in a world dominated by patronage based on class and complex social strata. Opportunity was often only open to those who belonged to the appropriate class or whose patrons were influential. As the adage goes, it wasn't what you knew but who you knew that opened doors of opportunity. Imagine then the strength of the "slave of Christ" metaphor in demonstrating the value of having a master who was the literal Son of God. Though the world did not recognize the power of that name, for those who had been converted, the name of Jesus Christ was everything that they could hope for because of its ability to bring the endless opportunity afforded by eternal life.

This may be part of the reasoning behind the scriptural emphasis on our belief "in" or "on" *the name* of Christ, as well as confidence that "through" the name of Christ we can be redeemed.[366]

Acts 4:10–12

Be it known unto you all, and to all the people of Israel, that by the name of Jesus Christ of Nazareth, whom ye crucified, whom God raised from the dead, even by him doth this man stand here before you whole. This is the stone which was set at nought of you builders, which is become the head of the corner. Neither is there salvation in any other: for there is none other name under heaven given among men, whereby we must be saved.

1 John 3:23

And this is his commandment, That we should believe on the name of his Son Jesus Christ, and love one another, as he gave us commandment.

John 1:11–12

He came unto his own, and his own received him not. But as many as received him, to them gave he power to become the sons of God, even to them that believe on his name.

John 20:31

But these are written, that ye might believe that Jesus is the Christ, the Son of God; and that believing ye might have life through his name.

Recognizing that throughout the scriptures the use of *Lord* generally refers to Jesus Christ, the number of corroborating scriptures expands further. For example, though he didn't specifically use Christ's name during his sermon to the Jews on the day of Pentecost, Peter was clearly referring to the saving power of the name of Jesus Christ.[367] Paul could have quoted either Peter or a number of Old Testament prophets[368] when he taught the Romans the same principle:

Romans 10:13

For whosoever shall call upon the name of the Lord shall be saved.

Peter's commitment to the concept that the name of Jesus Christ is the starting point for conversion to the gospel was illustrated by the account of the lame man at the gate of the temple.[369] The observant physician Luke noted that the man was crippled from his mother's womb and implied the pitiable deformity and atrophy that must have been present in this man who had never been able to walk.

Acts 3:6–8 (emphasis added)

Then Peter said, Silver and gold have I none; but such as I have give I thee: *In the name of Jesus Christ of Nazareth* rise up and walk. And he took him by the right hand, and lifted him up: and immediately his feet and ankle bones received strength. And he leaping up stood, and walked, and entered with them into the temple, walking, and leaping, and praising God.

Luke's amazement at the sheer magnitude of this miracle is clear by his description of the immediacy with which his atrophic and withered feet received their strength and allowed him to stand, walk, and leap with joy. Luke's words leave no doubt that, for Peter (and presumably John and Luke), it was the name of Christ and faith in His name that saved the cripple:

Acts 3:16

And [Jesus Christ's] name through faith in his name hath made this man strong, whom ye see and know: yea, the faith which is by him hath given him this perfect soundness in the presence of you all.

Though required to look up to Peter and John as he begged for his living,[370] his deliverance from bondage came only as he looked with the eye of faith to Jesus Christ. This faith, and the all-powerful name of his new master, was able to heal his body and save his soul.

One of the most important things we do every week is witness to God at that we are willing to take upon us the name of Christ as we partake the sacrament. This helps us to remember Him and to keep His commandments. In doing so, we recommit ourselves to be enslaved to Him. We submit our will to His, desiring only to do His will. Then, slowly and almost imperceptibly, we find that this process of taking on His name helps us understand who we really are. And, most important of all, we find our hearts are changed by Christ's name.

Chapter 9: Setting the Captive Free

After His baptism by John, Jesus returned to Galilee, where He formally began His ministry. One of the first recorded details of this ministry transpired in His home synagogue in Nazareth. Taking up the scriptures, He stood before His neighbors and read the sixy-first chapter of Isaiah.[371]

Luke 4:18–21

The Spirit of the Lord is upon me, because he hath anointed me to preach the gospel to the poor; he hath sent me to heal the brokenhearted, to preach deliverance to the captives, and recovering of sight to the blind, to set at liberty them that are bruised, to preach the acceptable year of the Lord. And he closed the book, and he gave it again to the minister, and sat down. And the eyes of all them that were in the synagogue were fastened on him. And he began to say unto them, This day is this scripture fulfilled in your ears.

Jesus was there to redeem His people and liberate them from their bondage, regardless of how unaware they were of their own captivity. There can be no doubt that He knew the nature of His mission and of its immense, eternal importance. While truly astounded by the grace of his words,[372] the people of Nazareth could not get beyond the fact that this was the Jesus they had watched grow from a boy. Instead of greeting Him as their long-awaited savior, they were filled with rage and even went so far as to try to kill Him.[373]

This account confirms that, though He was the creator of heaven and earth and the Son of God, He was limited in His ability to redeem those who were captive by their lack of faith: "he could there do no might work, save that he laid his hands upon a few sick folk, and healed them."[374] To grant His people eternal freedom required their consent.

Paul often spoke of the freedom that comes from Christ. Perhaps his role as the Apostle of freedom[375] came from his awareness of his own captivity to sin and the ensuing joy he experienced after being freed. At any rate, after the road to Damascus, Paul was acutely aware of his own need for a savior and his responsibility to make the liberty of Christ available to all men.

Romans 8:2

For the law of the Spirit of life in Christ Jesus hath made me free from the law of sin and death.

Anciently, there were two ways a master's name could grant freedom to a slave. The first was through manumission. The second was through adoption. These avenues to freedom are alluded to in the teachings of the New Testament in conjunction with the "slaves of Christ" metaphor.

Manumission

For the majority of slaves, freedom came through manumission. As slaves, they were considered part of their masters' family. As freedmen, they remained under the sphere of influence of the masters and were still closely identified with them. The freedmen became the clients and the former masters their patrons. As they gained their freedom, they were usually given their peculium, plus a small inheritance from their masters. Frequently, they were also given the masters' assistance in business ventures.

Though now free, slaves were dependent on their former master for protection and sustenance. The freedmen had duties and responsibilities towards their masters. In turn, masters acted as patrons and provided protection, support, and opportunities. In many cases, they were also tied together through their business ventures and joint partnerships.[376]

There was a *de facto* bond of freedman with his or her former master. The identity of the freedman was tied to the name of the former master in a way that transcended death. This is evidenced by many funerary inscriptions of the time. After death, the manumitted slaves identified themselves on their tombstones by inscribing their names, followed by "freedman (*apeleutheros*) of [patron's name]."[377]

The Atonement represents the ultimate patronage, with Christ as the great patron and us being His clients who are so completely dependent on the good graces of the patron. In the patronal society of the Roman world, this would have been a powerful teaching opportunity.

For example, Paul found that the Corinthians Saints were a widely diverse group. Some were converted as slaves, though a great many of them were freeborn. Some had nothing, while others were prosperous and fantastically wealthy. But all of them needed to be unified in their faith and understand more completely the Atonement of Christ.

1 Corinthians 7:22–23

For he that is called in the Lord, being a servant [*doulos*], is the Lord's freeman [*apeleutheros*]: likewise also he that is called, being free [*eleutheros*], is Christ's servant [slave]. Ye are bought with a price; be not ye the servants of men.

Paul's juxtaposition of the Greek words *apeleutheros* (a manumitted slave)[378] and *eleutheros* (a freeborn man)[379] simultaneously spoke of the varied needs of a highly diverse church. Additionally, it demonstrated his mastery of the most sophisticated rhetorical tools of the time, which allowed him to "comfort the afflicted, and afflict the comfortable."[380] To the Corinthian Saints who were literal slaves (*doulos*), Paul comforted them in the knowledge that through the gospel, they became "the Lord's freeman" (*apeleutheros kurios*). He connected with them by speaking to their yearnings for freedom. He showed how the gospel offered spiritual freedom. As slaves of men, they could never know the blessings of being freeborn, but as slaves to Christ, they could enjoy spiritual manumission. With that emancipation also came the opportunity afforded them as the client of their patron, Jesus Christ.

Likewise, Paul counseled the freeborn (*eleutheros*) Corinthians. Lest they took pride in their worldly freedoms and forget, he reminded them that Christ ransomed them from the slavery of sin. As a result, though free, the freeborn were Christ's slaves.

To encounter a freedman was an everyday occurrence in the Roman world. By his use of the phrase *freedman of the Lord*, Paul emphasized Christ's ability to free people from the bonds of slavery and sin. To be a freedman of the Lord was to have liberty, but also enjoy the esteem, status, and benefits associated with the Master's name and reputation. It was a promise that held equal appeal to the lowest of Corinthian slaves and the wealthiest of aristocrats.

This was the knowledge that could bring about "the unity of the faith"[381] Paul spent his life trying to entrench in the churches of Asia:

Galatians 3:26–28

For ye are all the children of God by faith in Christ Jesus. For as many of you as have been baptized into Christ have put on Christ. There is neither Jew nor Greek, there is neither bond nor free, there is neither male nor female: for ye are all one in Christ Jesus.

Adoption

The institution of adoption has existed from the earliest times in recorded history. The Abrahamic covenant, in which literal and adoptive children of Abraham are promised great gospel blessings, is one of the earliest doctrines of the Old Testament.[382] *The Code of Hammurabi* detailed laws regarding adoption in the Babylonian Empire from the eighteenth century BC. The book of Exodus outlined the adoption of Moses by the daughter of Pharaoh, thereby making it part of the Israelite tradition.[383] It existed throughout the Greco-Roman world. Justinian codified Roman laws regarding adoption in the sixth century AD with *The Institutes*.[384] Like marriage or divorce or slavery, it was a part of every culture.

Adoption served many purposes. Much like marriage was used to create ties between families, adoption was employed in much the same way. Because adoption did not necessarily abolish the relationship of a child with the biological family, it could be used to strategically bind families together. This was particularly common among the noble families of the Roman Empire.[385] It could therefore be an effective tool for social or political advancement and serve to ensure the upward mobility of a child. It was usually accompanied by exchange of money among the Roman nobility.

On a more practical level, adoption was used to secure a suitable male heir when there wasn't a biological one (or if the heir-apparent did not meet the standards of the *pater familias*). Finally, it could be used as a strategy to ensure the care and maintenance of a couple in old age. The adopted child (frequently a slave) was brought into the family with contractual obligations to care for the adoptive parents in their old age and appropriately mourn them and attend to funerary rites upon their deaths.[386]

There are many examples of a father willingly giving his son up for adoption. The adopted child took the name, status, and honor of the adoptive father, not the biological father. A plebian child adopted by a patrician family became a patrician. One renowned example of this is the posthumous adoption of Gaius Octavius Thurinus by his great uncle Gaius Julius Caesar. Thereafter, he became Gaius Julius Caesar Augustus and became the first—and greatest—emperor of the Roman Empire. In acknowledging his rival's timely adoption in Roman history, Marc Antony said, "You, boy, owe everything to a name."[387] Likewise, adoption was a frequently used tool to ensure imperial succession, with Tiberius, Caligula, Nero, Trajan, and Hadrian representing some of those who became emperor through adoption.

In the first-century Church, there were two ways to have children: by conceiving them in legitimate wedlock or by adoption. Adoption was frequently used to emancipate slaves and offer them the status and legitimacy of the family. The children born to a female slave were likewise slaves, unless the father adopted them as children. Adoption therefore represented an avenue to emancipation from slavery that was every bit as viable as freedom through manumission. To miss this context—in which the institution of adoption was framed—is to miss the rationale for so many references to adoption as a cherished fruit of the gospel for the early Saints.

To the Jews, the idea of adoption through the Abrahamic covenant held great theological significance. It was a source of national pride, whereby the Jews counted Abraham as their father.[388] This genealogy, whether by direct bloodlines or through adoption, was central to the Jewish concept of who they were and how God would save them.

Prior to his martyrdom, Stephen described the life of Moses as a type of Christ. Born as the son of Hebrew slaves in Egypt, Moses entered this world as a slave. From this humble beginning, he found himself adopted into the family of the king of Egypt. To him was afforded every blessing and opportunity as the son of royalty. Through him, God spoke and ultimately delivered the Hebrew people from the bondage of slavery.[389] We readily see in Moses a foreshadowing of Christ. But the story of Moses is also an archetype of the promises afforded by the adoption of sons. Because of these perspectives, adoption was also a ready institution that the Church leaders could use as a teaching tool.

Paul used the concept of adoption and the Abrahamic covenant to rescue the wayward Galatians. It was a particularly useful strategy to reclaim those who had been Jews prior to their conversion. The line between Judaism and Christianity, though bright from our perspective today, was not so clear in the early Church. The law had correctly been cherished as a great gift from God to His people and had dominated every aspect of Jewish life throughout the Holy Land and Diaspora.

The Epistle to the Galatians was Paul's attempt to try and correct the tendency of some Saints to return to the law of Moses—like dropping out of a university and returning to a favorite grade-school teacher. He taught that "Christ hath redeemed us from the curse of the law."[390] In a real sense, it was not only sin that enslaved them. They were equally enslaved by their adherence to a law that had been fulfilled in Christ. Paul taught that we become "sons" through faith in Jesus Christ. After being baptized "into Christ," we become His family and are therefore "heirs according to the promise."[391]

Paul went on to say that, from a practical perspective, children were like slaves. In all things, they are subject to those in authority over them. Though they would one day be masters of the house, for now they were in bondage. Like children, the Saints were once in bondage. For many, it was to sin; for some, it was to the law. In both cases, Christ redeemed them and offered them the freedom that comes through adoption into the family of God.[392]

Galatians 4:5–7

[Christ came] to redeem them that were under the law, that we might receive the adoption of sons. And because ye are sons, God hath sent forth the Spirit of his Son into your hearts, crying, Abba, Father. Wherefore thou art no more a servant, but a son; and if a son, then an heir of God through Christ.

As we realize this great blessing, we then have courage to "stand fast therefore in the liberty wherewith Christ hath made us free, and be not entangled again with the yoke of bondage,"[393] whether it was in the bondage of sin or the bondage of the law of Moses.

To any who have felt the joy of repentance and forgiveness, the yoke of bondage is a fearsome prospect. And it's a yoke to which every Christian returns—even if temporarily. The eighth chapter of Romans is Paul's attempt to quell such fears. Somehow, we all tend to forget that "the Spirit of life in Christ Jesus hath made [us] free from the law of sin and death."[394] Paul described the yoke of sin as "the spirit of bondage," leaving us crippled with self-loathing and fear.[395] Yet, by remembering our Savior, we remember,

Romans 8:15–17

[We] have received the Spirit of adoption, whereby we cry, Abba, Father. The Spirit itself beareth witness with our spirit, that we are the children of God: and if children, then heirs; heirs of God, and joint-heirs with Christ.

Though the afflictions of the world will cause us to suffer and groan under the effects of pain and temptation, we need not fear as we wait for the promises and fruits of the adoption to take place. We can have confidence that we "shall be delivered from the bondage of corruption into the glorious liberty of the children of God."[396] We look forward to the great gifts[397] He has promised to those once captive. We patiently await the day when God "shall wipe away all tears from [our] eyes; and there shall be no more death, neither sorrow, nor crying, neither shall there be any more pain." Truly we will call Him "Father," for He "will be [our] God, and [we] shall be [His sons]."[398]

The crowning element of the "slave of Christ" metaphor lies in the promise that Christ's slaves will one day be adopted as God's sons.[399] By believing in Him, we become God's sons[400] and heirs to all that our Father in Heaven has.[401]

Chapter 10: Freedom by Voluntary Enslavement

Levitical Law required the mandatory manumission of slaves after six years.[402] Yet it also acknowledged that some slaves did not want to leave their masters. In such cases, there was an established practice by which the slave promised love and fealty to the master and a desire to serve him forever.[403] In return, the master had certain specific responsibilities to the slave and his or her family.

This covenant had to be executed before judges, for it represented voluntary, continuous enslavement of the slave to a master. The master formalized the ceremony by piercing the ear of the slave with an awl. The needle, as it passed through the upper portion of the right ear, then penetrated into the wood of the door or doorpost of the master's home. It was a ceremony that had to be done by the master; it could not be delegated to a son or messenger.

> The ear is a hieroglyphic of obedience, and the boring of it through to the doorpost denotes the strict and close obedience of such a servant to his master, and how he is, and ought to be, addicted to his service, and be constantly employed in it, and never stir from it, nor so much as go over the threshold of his master's house.[404]

The highly symbolic nature of the ceremony is obvious. The slave became figuratively (and literally) attached to that household. He was bound to hear all the master's orders and to obey them punctually.[405] The ceremony left graphic evidence of voluntary, lifelong slavery to the master and his house. It served to remind master, slave, and any onlooker of the covenant. It's intriguing to wonder if Paul had this ceremony in mind when he said, "I bear in my body the marks of the Lord Jesus Christ."[406]

Christian converts who were formerly Jews may have recognized similarities between this ancient ceremony and the ordinance of baptism. Baptism was also a carefully prescribed ceremony. It had to be performed in the presence of witnesses and could only be done by "one having authority." In the baptismal ordinance, the convert is buried in the water and willingly gives up his or her old life to become permanently attached to the household of Christ.

Ephesians 2:19

Now therefore ye are no more strangers and foreigners, but fellow-citizens with the saints, and of the household of God.

The parallels between slaves kneeling before the master to have their ears pierced and attached to the doorpost and slaves of Christ kneeling before the Redeemer and promising lifelong service are obvious. It is staggering to consider that a slave would have loved and trusted a master so much that he or she would unconditionally surrender life and will to another person. This is particularly true when the relationship (physical slavery) was often prone to abuse. For the metaphorical slaves of Christ, there is nothing to lose and everything to gain by lifelong commitment to the Master.

The need for voluntary enslavement and surrender of our will to God is one more paradox in the larger "slave of Christ" metaphor, especially when we consider that we are not slaves by choice in the first place. It has already been demonstrated that Christ's instructions to the Apostles at the Last Supper strongly emphasized the involuntary nature of their calls to be slaves: "Ye have not chosen me, but I have chosen you."[407] But He also taught that the will of the slave is indispensible in the concept of the faithful slave. His disciples were repeatedly reminded to surrender their wills to God by taking up their crosses and following Him.[408] Similarly, His invitation to take up His yoke also implies the willing surrender, or consent of the disciple. None of us are slaves by choice, but rather we are slaves because of the nature of our redemption by Christ from the slavery of sin.

Yet in order to be faithful slaves, we must serve our Master with all our heart, might, mind, and strength. Our service must be voluntary, sincere, and unrestrained. Our will must be gladly surrendered to the will of the Master. It is implicit in the "slave of Christ" metaphor that willing obedience and faithful service are part of the duty we owe Him.

The story of Saint Patrick[409] is a truly awe-inspiring account of a young slave who was miraculously liberated by the power of God, only to voluntarily enslave himself to Christ after gaining his freedom.[410]

Though born to a Christian family in Roman Britain, Patrick stated that "he knew not the true God" when he was taken captive by Irish raiders at the age of sixteen,[411] along with thousands of his countrymen. His lot in life as their slave was among the most difficult imaginable.[412] Serving as a shepherd, he lived in the mountains and wood, with little to eat and no shelter from the incessant rain, wind, and cold. Speaking of enslavement, Patrick wrote, "Those who are kept in slavery suffer the most. They endure terrors and constant threats."[413]

Remembering the teachings of his father, he began to call on the name of God. The more he prayed, the more his love of God grew. He described a remarkable process in which his prayers fueled his faith. He was comforted and strengthened in his afflictions as he felt the love of God in his life.

After six years of slavery, God spoke to Patrick in a dream and told him that he would be free and was to then return to his homeland. He managed to escape and experienced repeated heavenly interventions that led him back to his home.

After being restored to his homeland and family, Patrick resolved that he would never leave them.[414] Yet, almost immediately, the Spirit began to call him to a greater purpose. He later wrote, "I never had any cause except the Gospel and his promises for ever returning to that nation from whence previously I scarcely escaped."[415] Patrick had dreams and visions of the inhabitants of Ireland begging him to return and he heard the voice of Jesus Christ calling him to share the gospel with those who had once made him a slave.[416] Being "nearly worn out" by the Spirit, he proceeded to Ireland to preach the gospel—this time of his own accord.[417] Though his mission to Ireland quickly ushered in a new round of insults, persecutions, and bonds,[418] he eventually found great success in sharing the gospel.[419]

Patrick recounted baptizing and confirming great numbers of Irish proselytes into the Christian faith.[420] The day after one such baptism, he was horrified to discover that the community had been attacked by British slave traders, who were themselves Christian. Soldiers under the command of Coroticus descended on Patrick's converts and cruelly slaughtered them in great numbers. Coroticus looted the town and took the survivors as slaves.[421] The Christian raiders jeered at Patrick's appeal for the return of the newly baptized Irish Saints. Patrick stated he didn't know who to lament more: the slain, the enslaved, or their captors—who he described as "slaves of hell," "bondservants of sin," and "son[s] of the devil."[422]

Patrick counseled the Saints to not associate with Coroticus or his men in any way[423] until they repented and made restitution by freeing those they'd taken as slaves. The prescribed restitution was a clever play on words: "liberate the servants[424] of God and the baptized handmaidens of Christ, for whom he died and was crucified."[425] In Patrick's mind, the newly baptized Saints of Ireland were already slaves to Christ when they were kidnapped and enslaved by Coroticus. For Patrick, conversion to the gospel and redemption by Jesus Christ redeemed the sinner from the enslavement of sin and simultaneously enslaved them to their new master—Jesus Christ.

Though Patrick's perspective as the one-time shepherd slave of an Irish master is fascinating, his views on enslavement to Christ are far more interesting and relevant. Patrick referred to his mission to Ireland as one of enslavement to Christ: "Who compelled me? I am bound in the Spirit not to see any one of my kinsfolk. . . . I was freeborn according to the flesh; I am born of a father who was a decurion; but I sold my noble rank—I blush not to state it, nor am I sorry—for the profit of others; in short, I am a slave in Christ to a foreign nation for the unspeakable glory of the eternal life which is in Christ Jesus our Lord."[426] Patrick referred to himself as God's poor servant, having suffered many great calamities and difficulties, having lived a life of slavery for many years. The line that delineated his mortal slavery to the Irish versus the many years of his spiritual enslavement to Christ as he labored among the Irish is almost impossible to define.[427]

The Apostasy had undoubtedly resulted in the loss of many plain and precious truths from the Church. The Apostasy was well under way when Patrick wrote his *Confession* and *Epistle*. Accordingly, Patrick's understanding of the gospel was different from that taught by Peter or Paul four hundred years earlier. But Patrick's view of conversion clearly illustrates that the concept of enslavement to Christ remained intact to a remarkable degree. There can be no doubt that he was one who willingly and completely enslaved himself to the Lord Jesus Christ, based on the light he was given at the time.

This kind of willing obedience is an important theme that spans all of the standard works. In reaching out to idolatrous Israel through the prophet Isaiah, Jehovah offered His people redemption. He required not simply perfunctory fulfillment of the law, but sincerity of heart.

Isaiah 1:18–20 (emphasis added)

Come now, and let us reason together, saith the Lord: though your sins be as scarlet, they shall be as white as snow; though they be red like crimson, they shall be as wool. If ye be *willing and obedient*, ye shall eat the good of the land: But if ye refuse and rebel, ye shall be devoured with the sword: for the mouth of the Lord hath spoken it.

Willing obedience is a universal requirement. As such, we see similar commandments from the Lord to His people across the centuries.

2 Nephi 31:14–15 (emphasis added)[428]

But, behold, my beloved brethren, thus came the voice of the Son unto me, saying: After ye have repented of your sins, *and witnessed unto the Father that ye are willing to keep my commandments*, by the baptism of water, and have received the baptism of fire and of the Holy Ghost, and can speak with a new tongue, yea, even with the tongue of angels, and after this should deny me, it would have been better for you that ye had not known me. And I heard a voice from the Father, saying: Yea, the words of my Beloved are true and faithful. He that endureth to the end, the same shall be saved.

D&C 20:37 (emphasis added)

All those who humble themselves before God, and desire to be baptized, and come forth with broken hearts and contrite spirits, and witness before the church that they have truly repented of all their sins, and *are willing to take upon them the name of Jesus Christ, having a determination to serve him to the end*, and truly manifest by their works that they have received of the Spirit of Christ unto the remission of their sins, shall be received by baptism into his church.

D&C 64:34–35 (emphasis added)

Behold, *the Lord requireth the heart and a willing mind; and the willing and obedient* shall eat the good of the land of Zion in these last days. And the rebellious shall be cut off out of the land of Zion, and shall be sent away, and shall not inherit the land.

As Jesus taught the parables of the talents[429] and the pounds,[430] He highlighted the critical nature of the slaves' faithfulness in determining their reward. A slave's only desire should be to please the master and carry out the master's will. Paul certainly was referring to this when he said, "Do I seek to please men? For if I yet pleased men, I should not be the servant [*doulos*] of Christ."[431] Paul knew that he only had one master.

Luke 16:13

No servant[432] can serve two masters: for either he will hate the one, and love the other; or else he will hold to the one, and despise the other. Ye cannot serve God and mammon.

There are certainly other instances in the New Testament in which we are taught that we become free when we willingly enslave ourselves to Jesus Christ's service. In Galatians 5:13, Paul speaks of men being "called unto liberty." The word translated as "call" is *kaleō*,[433] and means "to name, by name," "to give a name to," or "to bear a name or title." Hence, Paul's words could read "we are named to be free" and should therefore love and serve one another rather than serve the trappings of the flesh. Our newly given name, slave of Jesus Christ, defines us.

Along a similar vein, Peter described the motivations of the Saints after being ransomed by Jesus Christ. He stated that we do not use our freedom for evil motives, but rather hold this freedom in our willing enslavement of God.[434] And for the Church located at Thessalonica, Paul reiterated they were not dragged away from the worship of their idols. Rather, of their own volition, they turned away and served the living God.[435]

Consider the Greek word *douloō*, which is variably translated as "bondage" or "servant" in the New Testament. The original Greek word suggests voluntary, willful enslavement in most contexts.[436] For example, Paul used this word in speaking of himself, a freeborn Roman citizen, who chose to be a slave to all for Christ's sake:

1 Corinthians 9:19

For though I be free from all men, yet have I made myself servant [*douloō*] unto all, that I might gain the more.

Similarly, he used *douloō* in the sixth chapter of Romans to refer to the terms of our servitude to Christ after our ransom.[437] As a result, we should not only be willing but also eager to yield ourselves to God rather than to sin. Paul spoke of our obedience "from the heart,"[438] as well as our service "with the mind,"[439] to characterize Christ's faithful slaves.

Romans 6:16–18

Know ye not, that to whom ye yield yourselves servants to obey, his servants ye are to whom ye obey; whether of sin unto death, or of obedience unto righteousness? But God be thanked, that ye were the servants of sin, but ye have obeyed from the heart that form of doctrine which was delivered you. Being then made free from sin, ye became the servants [*douloō*] of righteousness.

Romans 6:22

But now being made free from sin, and become servants [*douloō*] to God, ye have your fruit unto holiness, and the end everlasting life.

In 1 Corinthians 9:27, Paul used the term *doulagōgeō*—a derivation of *doulos*—to describe the process of subjugating the body's passions as we develop temperance and self-mastery. *Doulagōgeō* is translated as "to lead away into slavery; to make a slave and treat as a slave."[440] In this context, Paul is the one who has enslaved his will and surrendered it to the will of his Lord. He taught the Saints these same principles. It was essential to "[bring] into captivity every thought to the obedience of Christ."[441] He also spoke of the need for self-imposed captivity of the body in the great war between the will and the flesh.[442] The faithful slave bridles his passions and the trappings of the flesh and surrenders his will to the Lord. He will gladly "present your bodies a living sacrifice, holy, acceptable unto God."[443]

The following passages herald back to this teaching of Christ.

John 12:24–26

Except a corn of wheat fall into the ground and die, it abideth alone: but if it die, it bringeth forth much fruit. He that loveth his life shall lose it; and he that hateth his life in this world shall keep it unto life eternal. If any man serve me, let him follow me; and where I am, there shall also my servant be: if any man serve me, him will my Father honour.

Just as a seed must die to live again and bring forth fruit, so it is that we must give away our lives and wills to God so we may live eternally and have eternal increase.[444] It's a matter of priorities; we must love God first and foremost. For a person to value his or her life and will above God is to lose the true life.[445] To love Christ above ourselves is to gain far more than we could ever hope for in a life devoted to self.[446]

The greatest example of voluntary enslavement to God is the Savior Himself. Jesus seemed to expect nothing less from His disciples and emphasized their willingness to do the Father's will, just as He had.[447] More than any other Gospel, the Gospel of John highlights that Jesus followed not His own agenda, but that of His Father. Jesus Christ was sent by the Father.[448] It was the Father's message, plan, and will that He sought to implement.[449] In light of this overarching theme in John's account, it is somewhat surprising that John does not recount Christ pleading with His Father in Gethsemane to remove the bitter cup of the Atonement. Instead, John recorded Christ's determination to submit Himself to the Father's will as He instructed Peter to put away his weapon after he assaulted Malchus.[450] This notwithstanding, we have uniform consensus among the Synoptic Gospels of Jesus's great moment of truth in the Garden of Gethsemane, "where eternity hung in the balance."[451]

Luke 22:41–44[452]

And he was withdrawn from them about a stone's cast, and kneeled down, and prayed, saying, Father, if thou be willing, remove this cup from me: nevertheless not my will, but thine, be done. And there appeared an angel unto him from heaven, strengthening him. And being in an agony he prayed more earnestly: and his sweat was as it were great drops of blood falling down to the ground.

Though he faced unspeakable pain and suffering in both body and mind, Jesus was faithful and humbly submitted His will to the will of His Master. He is the ultimate in obedience and faithfulness as a slave. Each week, we are asked to ponder this great event and make similar covenants as we partake of the sacrament.

D&C 20:77 (emphasis added)

O God, the Eternal Father, we ask thee in the name of thy Son, Jesus Christ, to bless and sanctify this bread to the souls of all those who partake of it, that they may eat in remembrance of the body of thy Son, and *witness unto thee*, O God, the Eternal Father, that *they are willing to take upon them the name of thy Son, and always remember him and keep his commandments which he has given them*; that they may always have his Spirit to be with them. Amen.

The sacrament is our covenant (and weekly reminder) of our willful enslavement to Christ. Though our ransom has already been paid, we must choose not to leave our Master. We trust Him; we love Him and should never be detached from His household or serve another. As we receive the ordinance of the broken bread, we figuratively kneel before Him. We promise to keep Him foremost in our thoughts and to always remember Him. We willingly accept the awl that marks us as His slaves for the rest of our lives. As we take on His name, we covenant to hear His commandments and gladly obey. We look forward to the inconceivably glorious blessings He has promised His good and faithful slaves.

Chapter 11: Faithful in All Things

At the end of it all, one may rightly ask if it really matters whether we see ourselves as being *servants* of Christ or *slaves* of Christ. Admittedly, both these scenarios make it possible to accept the gospel of Jesus Christ, embrace its saving ordinances and thereby become justified and sanctified through the Atonement of Jesus Christ. So long as we recognize our dependence on Him as our only source of redemption, it doesn't matter. After all, the social context in which we live and struggle through life's challenges is different from those of the first-century Mediterranean world.

Our existence today is worlds apart from that of the early Saints two thousand years ago. In spite of societal growth and expansion of our understanding of the world and man's place in it, we are in many ways similar to the Saints in Galatia, Rome, or Corinth at the time of Paul. The temptations we succumb to are fundamentally unchanged over thousands of years of scriptural warning. We remain vulnerable to the same passions, pride, selfishness, and trappings of the flesh. Life holds for both these times and people the full spectrum of experiences, from illness to health, pain to pleasure, and despair to joy.

In light of the things we share in common with the early Saints, we stand to benefit from the messages that strengthened their faith and firmed their resolve to keep the faith. Therefore, understanding the context in which Jesus and the early Church leaders spoke is extremely helpful in comprehending the message of the gospel.

And to this end, a more correct understanding of the slave versus servant concept is extremely helpful. After all, service has always been the hallmark of those who are converted to the gospel of Jesus Christ. For the Saints in the earliest days of Christianity, *service was slavery*. This perspective can help us understand what it means to be redeemed from sin, what it means to call Him Lord, and what it means to take upon us His name. It can be argued that understanding *service* in same context that the early Saints understood it will benefit us today—because we are still so much like them.

The elements of Christlike service are numerous, but they certainly embody the principles of willing obedience, willing surrender of our will to the will of our Master, and seeking foremost those things that will please Him. Coincidentally, these are also the attributes of the faithful slave. The blessings promised the faithful seem so much greater from the perspective of a slave, who has nothing and stands to gain freedom, adoption as a son of God, and become an heir to His kingdom.

We see shades of this understanding in the teachings of the Prophet Joseph Smith in his sixth *Lecture on Faith*. Though they are not regarded as revelation to the Church, these lectures are recognized as "profitable doctrine"[453] and represent a window into Joseph Smith's understanding of these matters.

> Let us here observe, that a religion that does not require the sacrifice of all things never has power sufficient to produce the faith necessary unto life and salvation; for, from the first existence of man, the faith necessary unto the enjoyment of life and salvation never could be obtained without the sacrifice of all earthly things. It was through this sacrifice, and this only, that God has ordained that men should enjoy eternal life; and it is through the medium of the sacrifice of all earthly things that men do actually know that they are doing the things that are well pleasing in the sight of God. When a man has offered in sacrifice all that he has for the truth's sake, not even withholding his life, and believing before God that he has been called to make this sacrifice because he seeks to do his will, he does know, most assuredly, that God does and will accept his sacrifice and offering, and that he has not, nor will not seek his face in vain. Under these circumstances, then, he can obtain the faith necessary for him to lay hold on eternal life.[454]

A great many critics of the Church have criticized this kind of faith as being blind. To encounter a people who not only wait on the words of a prophet, but also embrace them and follow them as if uttered by the Lord himself,[455] is beyond their understanding and smacks of mindless fanaticism. But for someone who has been lost and found again,[456] or has been dead and now is alive again,[457] it is no such thing. After wretched existences as slaves of sin, our ransom by Christ is sweet, causing us to joyfully proclaim to Him:

Mosiah 5:5

We are willing to enter into a covenant with our God to do his will, and to be obedient to his commandments in all things that he shall command us, all the remainder of our days.

Whether we call it slavery to Christ, as the early Saints did, or call it dedicating our lives to the service of Jesus Christ and His Church, it is part of the process of willingly sacrificing everything for God. It is the voluntary surrender of will; an act of complete trust and enduring love for our Lord and Master. It is part of the process that builds within us the faith we need to lay claim to the blessings of exaltation. It is an essential step whereby we realize that, in the end, we are no longer slaves, but rather have become eternally free.

Bibliography

1. Angela, Alberto. *A Day in the Life of Ancient Rome*. Translated by G. Conti. New York: Europa Editions, 2009.

2. Bradley, Keith. *Slavery and Society at Rome*. Cambridge: Cambridge University Press, 1994.

3. Brewer, E. C. "Yoke." *Dictionary of Phrase and Fable*. Philadelphia: Henry Altemus, 1898.

4. Brown, Raymond E. *An Introduction to the New Testament.* New York: Doubleday, 1996.

5. Card, Michael. *A Better Freedom: Finding Life as Slaves of Christ.* Downer's Grove, IL: Intervarsity Press, 2009.

6. Chapman, David W. *Ancient Jewish and Christian Perceptions of Crucifixion*. Grand Rapids, MI: Baker Publishing Group, 2010.

7. Cohen, Shaye J. D. *From the Maccabees to the Mishnah*. Second edition. Louisville: Westminister John Knox Press, 2006.

8. Combes, I. A. H. *The Metaphor of Slavery in the Writings of the Early Church From the New Testament to the Beginning of the Fifth Century*. Sheffield: Sheffield University Press, 1998.

9. Dabbs, Matthew D. *The Use of Rhetoric in Philemon: Background and Structure*. Retrieved 2 February 2011 from *The Use of Rhetoric*

in Philemon: Background and Structure. http://mattdabbs.files.wordpress.com/2009/03/rhetoric-in-philemon.pdf.

10. De Vaux, Roland. *Ancient Israel: Its Life and Institutions.* Grand Rapids, MI: Wm. B. Eerdmans Publishing, 1997.

11. Edersheim, Alfred. *Sketches of Jewish Social Life*. Updated edition. Peabody, MA: Hendrickson Publishers, Inc, 1994.

12. Edersheim, Alfred. *The Life and Times of Jesus the Messiah.* Updated edition. Peabody, MA: Hendrickson Publishers, Inc, 2009.

13. Farrar, Frederic W. *The Life of Christ.* Salt Lake City: Bookcraft, 1994.

14. Fitzmyer, Joseph A. *The Letter to Philemon: A New Translation.* Volume 34C. New York: Doubleday, 2000.

15. Galen. *On the Passions and Errors of the Soul.* Translated by P. W. Harkins. Columbus: Ohio State University Press, 1963.

16. Glancy, Jennifer A. *Slavery in Early Christianity.* Oxford: Oxford University Press, 2002.

17. Grout, J. (1997–2000). *Roman Trivia Questions #7*. Retrieved 2010 йил 30-November from Encyclopedia Romana: http://penelope.uchicago.edu/~grout/encyclopaedia_romana/miscellanea/trivia/yoke2.html.

18. Harris, Murray J. *Slave of Christ: A New Testament Metaphor for Total Devotion to Christ*. Edited by D. A. Carson. *New Studies in Biblical Theology 8*. Downer's Grove, IL: Intervarsity Press, 1999.

19. Hengel, Martin. *Crucifixion in the Ancient World and the Folly of the Message of the Cross.* Philadelphia: Fortress Press, 1977.

20. Josephus, Flavius. *The Works of Josephus*. New Updated Edition. Translated by William Whiston. Peabody, MA: Hendrickson Publishers, Inc, 1987.

21. Lewis, C. S. *The Screwtape Letters*. From *The Complete C. S. Lewis Signature Classics.* New York: Harper Collins, 2007.

22. MacArthur, John. *Slave.* Nashville, TN: Thomas Nelson, 2010.

23. Martin, Dale B. *Slavery as Salvation: The Metaphor of Slavery in Pauline Christianity.* New Haven, CT: Yale University Press, 1990.

24. Munro, Winsome. *Jesus, Born of a Slave: The Social and Economic Origins of Jesus' Message.* Studies in the Bible and Early Christianity. Vol. 37. Edwin Mellen Pr., 1998.

25. Northcote, J. S. *Epitaphs of the Catacombs or Christian Inscriptions in Rome During the First Four Centuries.* London: Longman, Green & Company, 1878.

26. Paulissian, Robert. "Adoption in Ancient Assyria and Babylonia." *Journal of Ancient Assyrian Academic Studies, 13.2*, 1999, 5–34.

27. Plautus. *Amphitryon.* Translated by L. Casson. New York: W. W. Norton & Co, 1971.

28. Plutarch. *Plutarch's Lives.* Vol. 3. Translated by A. Stewart & G. Long. London: Wm Clowes & Sons Ltd, 1892.

29. Rosner, Brian S. "The Concept of Idolatry." *Themelios 24.3*, 1999, 21–30.

30. Schiffman, Lawrence H. *From Text to Tradition.* Hoboken, NJ: Ktav Publishing House, 1991.

31. Skinner, Andrew C. *Gethsemane.* Salt Lake City: Deseret Book, 2002.

32. Talmage, James E. *Jesus the Christ.* Classics in Mormon Literature edition. Salt Lake City: Deseret Book, 1982.

33. Veyne, Paul (editor). *A History of Private Life, Volume 1: From Pagan Rome to Byzantium.* Cambridge, MA: Harvard University Press, 1992.

34. White, Newport J. D. *A Translation of the Latin Writings of St. Patrick.* London: The Society for Promoting Christian Knowledge, 1918.

35. White, Newport J. D. *Libri Sancti Patricii—The Latin Writings of St. Patrick.* Dublin: The University Press, 1905.

36. Yeivin, Z. A. "Yoke." In Michael Berenbaum (editor). *Encyclopedia Judaica.* Second Edition. Vol. 21. Detroit: Macmillian Reference, 2007, 381.

Endnotes

1. Luke 1:38.
2. Luke 1:48.
3. Luke 2:29.
4. Matthew 14:2.
5. John 15:15; 18:36.
6. Philippians 2:7.
7. Matthew 10:24; 20:27; 23:11; Mark 9:35; 10:44; John 13:16; 15:20.
8. Examples are far too numerous to recite, but see: Romans 1:1 (Paul); Colossians 4:12 (Epaphras); Philemon 1:25 (Onesimus); Hebrews 3:5 (Moses); James 1:1 (James); 2 Peter 1:1 (Simon Peter); Jude 1:1 (Jude); Revelation 1:1 (John); Philippians 1:1 (Paul and Timothy); Acts 2:18 (Saints on the day of Pentecost); Acts 4:25 (King David); Acts 4:29 (Peter and John); Acts 16:17 (Paul, Silas, and Luke); and Romans 16:1, 27 (Phebe).
9. The eighth article of faith states: "We believe the Bible to be the word of God as far as it is translated correctly; we also believe the Book of Mormon to be the word of God."

10. Keith Bradley, *Slavery and Society at Rome* (Cambridge, United Kingdom: Cambridge University Press, 1994), 152.

11. See Murray J. Harris, *Slave of Christ: A New Testament Metaphor for Total Devotion to Christ* (Downer's Grove, IL: Intervarsity Press, 1999); Michael Card, *A Better Freedom: Finding Life as Slaves of Christ* (Downer's Grove, IL: Intervarsity Press, 2009); Raymond E. Brown, *An Introduction to the New Testament* (New York: Doubleday, 1996), 67.

12. Joseph Smith—History 1:12.

13. Blue Letter Bible, "Dictionary and Word Search for *despotēs* (*Strong's 1203*)," 1996–2011, 8 April 2011, http://www.blueletter bible.org/lang/lexicon/lexicon.cfm?Strongs=G1203&t= KJV.

14. Blue Letter Bible, "Dictionary and Word Search for *doulos* (*Strong's 1401*)," 1996–2011, 8 April 2011, http://www.blueletter bible.org/lang/lexicon/lexicon.cfm?Strongs=G1401&t= KJV.

15. The word *despotes* is translated as "Lord" in this case, but it's the same word that is repeatedly used in Peter's epistles (1 Peter 2:18; 2 Peter 2:1) and several Pauline Epistles (1 Timothy 6:1–2; 2 Timothy 2:21; Titus 2:9) to refer to the relationship between a slave and a master. *Despotes* appears ten times in the KJV and is translated as "Lord" and "master" equally. In contrast, *kyrios* appears 744 times in the New Testament and is translated as "Lord" (667), "lord" (54), "master" (11), "sir" (6), and "Sir" (6).

16. There are two Hebrew words that are translated as "handmaid": *amah* and *shiphchah*. Though both words may be used to indicate a maid or domestic, most usages in the Old Testament relate to a bondwoman, a slave girl, a female slave, or a concubine. (Blue Letter Bible. "Dictionary and Word Search for *handmaid* in the KJV," 1996–2011, 8 April 2011, http://www.blueletterbible.org/search/translationResults.cfm? Criteria=handmaid&t=KJV.)

17. Luke 1:38. See also Raymond E. Brown, *An Introduction to the New Testament*, 67.

18. Luke 1:48.

19. Colossians 4:14. Paul refers to Luke as *agapetos iatros*, meaning "the beloved physician."

20. Paul's Epistles to the Thessalonians (AD 49), Galatians (AD 51), and Corinthians (AD 55), as well as the Gospel of Mark (AD 70), pre-date the Gospel of Luke and the Acts of the Apostles, which were written between AD 85 and 95.

21. Blue Letter Bible, "Dictionary and Word Search for *servant* in the KJV," 1996–2011, 8 April 2011, http://www. blueletterbible. org/search/translationResults.cfm?Criteria=servant&t=KJV.

22. S. J. Cohen, *From the Maccabees to the Mishnah*, second edition (Louisville, KY: Westminister John Knox Press, 2006), 156.

23. Josephus, *Antiquities of the Jews*, 13.10.6.

24. Lawrence H. Schiffman, *From Text to Tradition*, Hoboken, NJ: Ktav Publishing House, 1991), 3; 18 July 2011, http://cojs.org/ cojswiki/Pharisees_and_Sadducees.

25. Brown, *An Introduction to the New Testament*, 146, footnote 50.

26. S. J. Cohen, *From the Maccabees to the Mishnah*, second edition (Louisville, KY: Westminister John Knox Press, 2006), 152; see also Josephus, *Antiquities of the Jews*, 13.10.6.

27. Matthew 22:16; Mark 3:6; 12:13.

28. Schiffman, *From Text to Tradition*, 6–7.

29. Ibid., 4.

30. Frederic W. Farrar, *The Life of Christ* (Salt Lake City: Bookcraft, 1994), 591–94, footnote 2.

31. Josephus, *Antiquities of the Jews*, 13.10.6.

32. The link between societal stature and authority was so firmly entrenched in the minds of the ruling elite of this time that they marveled at the boldness of Peter and John in claiming authority from God. Though they claimed this authority and

performed great miracles, they were uneducated commoners with forgettable family pedigrees and no political connections (see Acts 4:7–14).

33. Luke 3:2; John 18:13, 24; Acts 4:6.

34. Farrar, *The Life of Christ*, 591.

35. Euripedes, *Ion*, 854.

36. Martin Hengel, *Crucifixion in the Ancient World and the Folly of the Message of the Cross* (Philadelphia: Fortress Press, 1977), 59.

37. Jennifer A. Glancy, *Slavery in Early Christianity* (Oxford: Oxford University Press, 2002), 7.

38. One denarius was a laborer's wage for one day's work.

39. Harris, *Slave of Christ*, 34.

40. See Glancy, *Slavery in Early Christianity*, 9, for a description of a bronze slave collar—complete with a cross—ordered by a fourth- or fifth-century Christian leader named Felix.

41. Slaves were frequently granted the right to earnings called a *peculium*. These funds technically belonged to the master and could be revoked at any time but were granted to slaves often, with the intent of being used to purchase their own freedom or for personal use. It was not unheard of for wealthy slaves of high-ranking Romans to buy other slaves (*servus vicarious*, or under-slaves) or to purchase the freedom of their common-law spouse (*contubernalis*) at the time of manumission.

42. Masters could grant slaves a form of common-law cohabitation called *contubernium*, but it was entirely based on the master's discretion and consent, and all children produced by such unions belonged to the master.

43. Dale B. Martin, *Slavery as Salvation: The Metaphor of Slavery in Pauline Christianity* (New Haven: Yale University Press, 1990), 2.

44. I. A. H. Combes, *The Metaphor of Slavery in the Writings of the Early Church from the New Testament to the Beginning of the Fifth Century* (Sheffield, England: Sheffield Academic Press, 1998), 22.

45. Glancy said that one of the most important sources of slaves for the slave market in Rome after the first century AD was natural reproduction, followed by rescue (and enslavement) of exposed children that parents chose to abandon. Some additional sources were prisoners of war, kidnapping, and even self-enslavement (see Glancy, *Slavery in Early Christianity*, 71–88). In the earlier part of the Roman Empire, war would have represented a more significant source of slaves for the Roman markets during the expansionist periods of the second and third centuries BC.

46. Bradley, *Slavery and Society at Rome*, 32.

47. Ibid., 26–27. See also Harris, *Slave of Christ*, 34.

48. Hengel, *Crucifixion in the Ancient World*, 46–50.

49. In this case, Julius Caesar was not sold into slavery, but rather held for a ransom of twenty talents. Caesar, though only a youth, mocked his captors for not recognizing his worth as a prisoner and voluntarily offered to give them fifty talents. He treated his captors with contempt and threatened to crucify them all. For thirty-eight days, Caesar acted more like their leader than their prisoner, joining in their games, composing poetry, and rehearsing speeches to his guards. When tired, he would even demand silence while he slept. After the ransom was paid, he raised a fleet of ships and made good on his earlier threats. He captured the pirates, took back his ransom, and crucified them all in Pergamum (see Plutarch, *The Life of Julius Caesar*, 1–2).

50. Glancy, *Slavery in Early Christianity*, 7–8.

51. Ibid., 4.

52. Bradley, *Slavery and Society at Rome*, 58–68; Glancy, *Slavery in Early Christianity*, 42–45.

53. Bradley, *Slavery and Society at Rome*, 62.

54. Hengel, *Crucifixion in the Ancient World*, 57–58.

55. Ibid., 58.

56. Ibid.

57. Ibid., 51–63.

58. For an extensive scholarly review of attitudes about crucifixion in the ancient Judeo-Christian world, see David W. Chapman, *Ancient Jewish and Christian Perceptions of Crucifixion* (Grand Rapids, MI: Baker Publishing Group, 2010).

59. Glancy, *Slavery in Early Christianity*, 21–24.

60. Paul Veyne (editor), *A History of Private Life from Pagan Rome to Byzantium* (Cambridge: Harvard University Press, 1987), 66.

61. Galen, O*n the Passions and Errors of the Soul*, translated by Paul W. Harkins (Ohio State University Press, 1963), 42.

62. Bradley, *Slavery and Society at Rome*, 166–67.

63. Glancy, *Slavery in Early Christianity*, 102.

64. "I do not wish to involve myself in too large a question, and to discuss the treatment of slaves, towards whom we Romans are excessively haughty, cruel, and insulting. But this is the kernel of my advice: Treat your inferiors as you would be treated by your betters. And as often as you reflect how much power you have over a slave, remember that your master has just as much power over you. 'But I have no master,' you say. You are still young; perhaps you will have one" (Seneca, *Moral Epistles*, 47.7).

65. Discourse 14.1, http://penelope.uchicago.edu/Thayer/E/Roman/Texts/Dio_Chrysostom/Discourses/14*.html.

66. Bradley, *Slavery and Society at Rome*, 155.

67. Glancy said that male slaves could expect manumission in their thirties and female slaves around menopause, so in their mid to late forties (Glancy, *Slavery in Early Christianity*, 17).

68. Harris, *Slave of Christ*, 39.

69. Martin, *Slavery as Salvation,* 8–9.

70. Blue Letter Bible, "Dictionary and Word Search for '*ebed (Strong's 5650),*" 1996–2011, 8 April 2011, http://www.blueletterbible.org/lang/lexicon/lexicon.cfm? Strongs=H5650&t=KJV.

71. Genesis 9:25–27.

72. Genesis 14:14: "And when Abram heard that his brother was taken captive, he armed his trained servants, born in his own house, three hundred and eighteen, and pursued them unto Dan." The Hebrew word translated as "born" can be translated as "(a slave) born in the house of his owner" (Geselnus's Lexicon, Blue Letter Bible Online).

73. For a detailed analysis, see Harris, *Slave of Christ*, 28–30.

74. Leviticus 25:39–55; Deuteronomy 15:12–18; Exodus 21:1–11, 20–21, 26–27, 32.

75. Deuteronomy 23:15–16.

76. Leviticus 25:39–40.

77. Deuteronomy 23:17–18.

78. For an extended discussion of the Hebraic tradition of slavery to God, see Combes, *The Metaphor of Slavery*, 42–48.

79. Leviticus 25:43.

80. Leviticus 25:54.

81. Deuteronomy 15:12–15.

82. Leviticus 25:48–49; see also the account of Boaz acting as Ruth's kindred redeemer in Ruth 2:20–4:14.

83. Glancy, *Slavery in Early Christianity*, 6–7.

84. Exodus 4:10.

85. Daniel 9:11; Malachi 4:4.

86. 1 Samuel 3:10.

87. Joshua 24:29.

88. 1 Kings 20:39; Isaiah 20:3.

89. Daniel 9:17.

90. Jeremiah 25:9; 26:5; 35:15; 44:4; Ezekiel 38:17; Daniel 9:6–10; Amos 3:7; Zechariah 1:6.

91. Jeremiah 33:21–22; Ezekiel 37:23–25.

92. Isaiah's "servant songs" refer to the Messiah as the Lord's slave (Isaiah 42:1–4; 49:1–6; 50:4–11; 52:13–53:12).

93. Isaiah 41:8–10. In this passage, Jehovah refers to the children of Israel as His slave (*'ebed*). Yet the Lord goes on to describe His relationship with Jacob, who was of the seed of Abraham, as His friend. He is more than just the master of a slave; He is their God. He has called them, chosen them, and would not reject them or cast them aside. Rather, He would abide with them, and strengthen and support them no matter what. The passage outlines a master-slave relationship, yet still emphasizes that, as their righteous and ever-loving master, He would never abandon them (see also Isaiah 44:1–2; 45:4). For additional Old Testament references to the children of Israel as God's slaves, see Leviticus 25:55; Jeremiah 30:10; 46:27–28; Ezekiel 28:25; 37:25.

94. Combes, *The Metaphor of Slavery*, 42–48.

95. Luke 1:38.

96. Luke 2:52.

97. For an extensive scholarly review of the theme of slavery in the parables and teachings of Jesus Christ, see Glancy, *Slavery in Early Christianity*, 102–29.

98. Card, *A Better Freedom*, 97, and Appendix D.

99. Winsome Munro, *Jesus, Born of a Slave: The Social and Economic Origins of Jesus' Message*, vol 37, Studies in the Bible and Early Christianity (Lewiston, NY: Edwin Mellen, 1998).

100. Luke 14:12–24.

101. Matthew 22:2–14.

102. Mark 12:1–12; Luke 20:9–19.

103. A slave's wife and children were not legally recognized as such, but they could be permitted according to the discretion of his master.

104. Matthew 18:23–35.

105. A slaveholder would often hire out the responsibility of slave punishment that involved torture or execution to *manceps*, a professional who earned a livelihood by torturing or executing slaves for a fee. See Glancy, *Slavery in Early Christianity*, 102.

106. John 8:32.

107. Matthew 13:24–30, 36–43.

108. Matthew 25:14–30.

109. Isaiah 41:8–10.

110. A. Edersheim, *The Life and Times of Jesus the Messiah* (Peabody, MA, USA: Hendrickson, 2009), 791 [2.460].

111. Bradley, *Slavery and Society at Rome*, 57–80.

112. The master "*delivered* unto them his goods" (Matthew 25:14; emphasis added). Thayer's Lexicon (Blue Letter Bible Online) indicates that the Greek word rendered as "delivered" (Strong's G3860—*paradidomi*) means "to give over into one's power or use, or in other words to deliver to one something to keep, use, take care of, manage."

113. Luke 12:48.

114. Edersheim, *The Life and Times of Jesus*, 793–94 [2.463–64].

115. Luke 19:11–27; also known as the parable of the minas, or the parable of the ten pieces of money.

116. Edersheim, *The Life and Times of Jesus*, 795–96 [2.466–67]; see also LDS Bible Dictionary "Parables" and Josephus, *Antiquities of the Jews*, 17:9.

117. Blue Letter Bible, "Dictionary and Word Search for *pragmateuomai (Strong's 4231)*," 1996–2011, 6 March 2011, http:// www.blue letterbible.org/lang/lexicon/lexicon.cfm? Strongs=G4231&t=KJV.

118. Josephus, *Antiquities of the Jews*, 17:11.

119. Edersheim, *The Life and Times of Jesus*, 791, 796 [2.460, 467].

120. Archaelaus had three thousand Jews slaughtered in the temple and its precincts when they rose up in protest of his usurpation of the throne during a religious festival (Josephus, *Antiquities of the Jews*, 17:9).

121. Luke 12:35–40.

122. Luke 12:41–48. A parallel but abbreviated account describing the wicked overseer is found in Matthew 24:42–51. It does not include the prior contrast with the faithful slaves awaiting the return of their master from the wedding, which is described in Luke 12.

123. Matthew 24:45; Luke 12:42.

124. Luke 17:7–10.

125. See also Jeremiah 2:20.

126. See Numbers 19:2; Deuteronomy 21:3.

127. Isaiah 14:25; 47:6.

128. Jeremiah 2:20; 27:8–15; 28:14; Lamentations 1:14; 3:27.

129. See Ezekiel 34:27, where Ezekiel speaks allegorically about the sheep (God's covenant people) that have been abandoned by the unrighteous shepherds of Israel (the kings of Israel and Judah, who led the people into idolatry, bringing about the Babylonian captivity through their unrighteousness).

130. Hosea 11:1–4; Nahum 1:13.

131. E. Cobham Brewer, "Yoke," *The Dictionary of Phrase and Fable* (Philadelphia: Henry Altemus, 1898); Bartleby.com, 2000, 30 November 2010.

132. J. Grout, *Roman Trivia Questions #7*, retrieved 30 November 2010 from Encyclopedia Romana: http://penelope.uchicago.edu/~grout/encyclopaedia_romana/miscellanea/trivia/yoke2.html.

133. Z. A. Yeivin, "Yoke," found in M. Berenbaum and F. Skolnik (eds), *Encyclopedia Judaica, 2nd Edition*, volume 21 (Detroit, MI: Macmillian Reference, 2007, 381); *Gale Virtual Reference Library*. Web. 29 November 2010. http://go.galegroup.com/ps/i.do?&id=GALE%7CCX2587521286&v=2.1&u=imcpl1111&it=r&p=GVRL&sw=w.

134. Harris, *Slave of Christ*, 93. See also *Mishna Avot*, 3:6: "Every one who takes upon himself the yoke of the law removes from his shoulders the yoke of government and daily sorrows. But whoever removes the yoke of the law will be burdened with the yoke of government and daily sorrows."

135. See Acts 15:10 and Galatians 5:1; Paul's first Epistle to Timothy refers to slaves as being under the yoke (1 Timothy 6:1).

136. Matthew 10:38; 16:24; Mark 8:34; 10:21; Luke 9:23; 14:27.

137. Hengel, *Crucifixion in the Ancient World*, 51–63.

138. Matthew 10:24; John 13:16; 15:20.

139. Matthew 10:24; 20:27–28; 23:11; Mark 9:35; 10:44.

140. John 12:24–26.

141. Harris, *Slave of Christ*, 51–52.

142. Luke 22:15.

143. Blue Letter Bible, "Dictionary and Word Search for *lention (Strong's 3012)*," 1996–2011, 19 June 2011, http://www.blueletterbible.org/lang/lexicon/lexicon.cfm?Strongs=G3012&t=KJV.

144. John 5:30; 8:29.

145. Matthew 26:39–42; Mark 14:36; Luke 22:42; John 18:11; Romans 15:3; Philippians 2:6–8.

146. John 15:15.

147. Acts 22:28; Romans 14:4.

148. It was common for physicians in the Roman Empire to be slaves who could later buy their freedom.

149. Ephesians 6:5–8; Colossians 3:22–25; Colossians 4:1; 1 Timothy 6:1; Titus 2:9; 1 Peter 2:18.

150. 1 Corinthians 1:11.

151. Combes, *The Metaphor of Slavery*, 52.

152. John Chrysostum (AD 349–407), who was the Archbishop of Constantinople, was known for his eloquent speaking and his insightful application of the scriptures to everyday life.

153. John Chrysostum, *Homiles on Ephesians*, 22.

154. Ibid., 22.

155. For a full translation of the text and Trajan's response, see: http://faculty.georgetown.edu/jod/texts/pliny.html.

156. Pliny, *Epistle*, 10.96–97.

157. It was common belief that refusal to give sacrifice to Roman gods would bring about their displeasure and vengeance upon the

entire Empire. It was simply not wise to provoke them. Rome tolerated the local religions of her conquered people so long as they also paid homage to the gods of Rome. Christians were unbending on this point. There was a long tradition of similar refusals by the Jews, but the Romans had a great love affair with things that were old. Judaism was ancient by Roman standards. Surprisingly, the Romans tolerated Jewish religious obstinacy to a greater degree—in spite of their history of insurrection. There were no extensive or systematic attempts to exterminate the Jewish religion. Christianity, on the other hand, was new; noncompliance was not tolerated.

158. Glancy, *Slavery in Early Christianity*, 130.

159. Pliny, *Epistle,* 10.96–97.

160. Ephesians 6:9 represents Paul's counsel to masters to improve in their treatment of their slaves.

161. Combes, *The Metaphor of Slavery*, 56–63. See also Martin, *Slavery as Salvation,* 8.

162. Bradley, *Slavery and Society at Rome*, 146–53. See also Combes, *The Metaphor of Slavery*, 64–67.

163. Paul was not imprisoned in a strict sense. He was under Roman guard and house arrest as he waited arraignment before Nero.

164. Philemon 1:24.

165. Colossians 4:9; 4:18.

166. Runaways were definitely damaged goods. A slave trader was obligated to say if a slave had a history of trying to escape. A captured slave would therefore have a much lower resale value at the auction block. Captured runaways therefore commonly found themselves being sold to the mines, galleys, gladiatorial arena, or other equally horrific fates.

167. Joseph A. Fitzmyer, *The Letter to Philemon*, the Anchor Bible, vol. 34C (New York: Doubleday, 2000), 18.

168. M. D. Dabbs, *The Use of Rhetoric in Philemon: Background and Structure*, retrieved on February 2, 2011 from *The Use of Rhetoric in Philemon: Background and Structure*, http://mattdabbs.files.wordpress.com/2009/03/rhetoric-in-philemon.pdf.

169. The KJV renders the words as *unprofitable* and *profitable*, but *useless* and *useful* are commonly used in other translations and are more in keeping with the meaning imparted by the slave name Onesimus.

170. Philemon 1:11, 13.

171. Colossians 4:1; Ephesians 6:9.

172. Blue Letter Bible, "Dictionary and Word Search for *sōma (Strong's 4983)*," 1996–2011, 8 April 2011, http://www.blueletterbible.org/lang/lexicon/lexicon.cfm?strongs=G4983.

173. Glancy, *Slavery in Early Christianity*, 10–11.

174. Harris, *Slave of Christ*, 107.

175. Seneca, *Moral Epistles*, 47.7.

176. Interested readers are referred to Henryk Sienkiewicz's classic historical fiction work *Quo Vadis*, which tells the story of the struggling Christian community under Nero. For his work, he was awarded the Nobel Prize for Literature in 1905.

177. Philippians 4:22; this probably referred to slaves and freedmen of Caesar who had joined the early Christian Church in Rome.

178. Seneca, *Moral Epistles*, 17.5, 47.7.

179. Harris, *Slave of Christ*, 52.

180. 2 Peter 2:19.

181. Romans 6:19, 23.

182. The KJV translates *doulos* as "servants" in Romans 6:19.

183. Titus 3:3.

184. Galatians 4:8.

185. Titus 2:3.

186. Galatians 5:1–4.

187. Hebrews 2:14–15.

188. Galatians 2:4.

189. Colossians 2:8.

190. Romans 7:14.

191. Romans 7:19.

192. 2 Timothy 2:26.

193. Luke 11:2–4; Matthew 6:9–13.

194. Luke 15:18–19, 21–24.

195. Matthew 9:2–8; Mark 2:5–12; Luke 5:18–25.

196. Luke 5:12–15; Luke 17:12–19.

197. Luke 13:11–17.

198. Mark 4:10–12; John 9:30–31, 39–41.

199. Luke 7:36–50.

200. How soon had they forgotten Egypt, Assyria, and Babylon!

201. For a contemporary discussion on enslaving power of addiction and sin, see M. Russell Ballard, "O That Cunning Plan of the Evil One" *Ensign*, November 2010.

202. "Texts involving the terms usually translated 'to serve' and 'to worship' supply unambiguous evidence that idolaters (and believers) were conceived of as serving and obeying their deities. Even in ceremonial contexts these words signify more than just isolated acts of cultic worship. When it is said that the people 'serve' Baal (Judges 10:6, 10, and so on) or other gods (Judges

10:13) or the Lord (Judges 10:16) the term implies not only the exclusive nature of the relationship but the total commitment and, in effect, obedience of the worshipper. That to 'serve' a deity involved doing their bidding is made clear in passages like Matthew 6:24 / Luke 16:13 where the 'service' is rendered to a master and the Pauline phrase 'bow the knee,' which is a synonym for worship." Brian Rosner, "The Concept of Idolatry," *Themelios* 24.3 (May 1999), 21–30 (27–28).

203. Matthew 6:24.

204. "Murder is no better than cards if cards can do the trick. Indeed the safest road to Hell is the gradual one—the gentle slope, soft underfoot, without sudden turnings, without milestones, without signposts."—C. S. Lewis, from *The Screwtape Letters* in *The Complete C. S. Lewis Signature Classics* (New York: Harper Collins, 2007) 220.

205. Bradley, *Slavery and Society at Rome*, 152.

206. Glancy, *Slavery in Early Christianity*, 96.

207. Joel 2:28–32.

208. Acts 2:18.

209. Acts 2:21; compare with Joel 2:32.

210. Acts 2:36.

211. The KJV translates *doulos* as "servant" in 2 Peter 1:1.

212. The KJV translates *doulos* as "servant" in Jude 1:1.

213. The KJV translates *doulos* as "servant(s)" in Revelation 1:1; 2:20; 7:3; 10:7; 11:18; 15:3; 19:2, 5; 22:3, 6.

214. The KJV translates *doulos* as "servant" in 2 Timothy 2:24.

215. 1 Corinthians 4:9–13 refers to the Apostles in such a way so as to evoke images of slaves in the gladiatorial arena, those who were destined to meet a violent death. Verse 9 states, "For I think

that God hath set forth us the apostles last, as it were appointed to death: for we are made a spectacle unto the world, and to angels, and to men." The word *spectacle* stems from *theatron* in Greek (Strong's G2302), indicating men who are exhibited to be gazed at and made sport of. The remaining verses similarly conjure up images of slavery being despised, hungry, thirsty, naked, buffeted, and without a dwelling place. They labor with their hands, are reviled and persecuted, are forced to suffer it, are defamed yet still entreat, and are made as the filth of the world.

216. The KJV translates *doulos* as "servant" in Acts 16:16–18.

217. The KJV translates *syndoulos* as "fellowservant" in Revelation 6:11; 19:10; 22:9.

218. The KJV translates *syndoulos* as "fellowservant" in Colossians 1:7; 4:7.

219. The Gospel of Thomas is a non-canonical work attributed to Judas Thomas. It discusses at length the relationship of Thomas as slave and Jesus Christ as his master.

220. Romans 1:1; Galatians 1:10; Philippians 1:1; Titus 1:1.

221. Acts 20:19 refers to Paul "serving the Lord with all humility of mind." The KJV translates *douleuo*, which means "be a slave," as "serving."

222. Galatians 6:17.

223. Blue Letter Bible, "Dictionary and Word Search for *stigma (Strong's 4742),*" 1996–2011, 6 February 2011, http://www.blueletterbible.org/lang/lexicon/lexicon.cfm?Strongs=G4742&t=KJV.

224. Acts 9:20–25; 17:1–10; 22:22–29; Galatians 1:17; 2 Corinthians 11:32–33.

225. Acts 14:19–20.

226. Acts 27:13–28:1.

227. Acts 16:16–25; 21:26–36.

228. The Sanhedrin: Acts 22:30–23:10; Felix: Acts 24:1–27; Festus: Acts 25:1–12; Agrippa: Acts 25:13–26:32.

229. 1 Corinthians 9:12–18; 2 Thessalonians 3:7–10; Acts 20:33–35.

230. Acts 18:1–3.

231. Paul represents a strong New Testament precedent for a truly "lay clergy" and reinforces the current use of a "lay clergy" in the Church today.

232. Martin, *Slavery as Salvation*, 69–70, 76–77.

233. Plato, *Republic*, 6.495; *Laws,* 5.741e.

234. Martin, *Slavery as Salvation*, 44–45.

235. 2 Corinthians 11:7; 2 Corinthians 12:13.

236. Martin, *Slavery as Salvation*, 83–84.

237. Blue Letter Bible, "Dictionary and Word Search for *oikonomia (Strong's 3622),*" 1996–2011, 8 April 2011, http://www.blueletterbible.org/lang/lexicon/lexicon.cfm?Strongs=G3622&t=KJV.

238. Martin, *Slavery as Salvation*, 68–75. See also Colossians 1:25.

239. Romans 1:16.

240. Acts 2:14–18.

241. Unlike Peter, Paul's Roman citizenship spared him the horrors of crucifixion. He received a more merciful form of execution.

242. Ephesians, Philippians, Colossians, and Philemon.

243. Ephesians 3:1; 4:1; Philemon 1:1, 9; 2 Timothy 1:8.

244. The captivity Epistles are similar in this regard to sections 121, 122, and 123 of the Doctrine and Covenants, which were given to Joseph Smith Jr. in Liberty Jail.

245. Philippians 1:7–8; Philemon 1:1, 9.

246. Colossians 4:18.

247. Philippians 3:8.

248. Colossians 1:23–25; Philippians 4:12–14.

249. Philippians 1:21–25.

250. Philippians 1:20.

251. Philippians 4:11–13.

252. "Those of Chloe" in 1 Corinthians 1:11.

253. 1 Corinthians 7:22; Ephesians 6:6; 1 Peter 2:16; Galatians 5:13; 2 Corinthians 4:5.

254. Ephesians 6:6. See also Hebrews 10:36; 1 Peter 4:2; 1 John 2:17 for similar teachings.

255. There is no evidence that this was the same Epaphroditus who was referred to in Philippians 2:25; 4:18. Epaphroditus was a common slave name, meaning "beloved of Aphrodite."

256. Origen, *Contra Celsum*, book 7 chapter LIII.

257. Epictetus, *The Discourses*, book 4, chapter 1.

258. Bradley, *Slavery and Society at Rome*, 174–175, 178. See also Epictetus, *The Discourses*, book 4, chapter 1.

259. Plautus, *Amphitryon*, translated by Lionel Casson (New York: W. W. Norton & Co, 1971), 165–70, 174–75.

260. Romans 3:23.

261. Romans 7:24.

262. Jeremiah 14:8; 17:13, Joel 3:16.

263. Deuteronomy 7:8; Isaiah 48:20; Psalm 34:15–19; Isaiah 52:3; Micah 6:4.

264. Compare with Mark 10:43–45.

265. Isaiah's "servant songs" refer to the Messiah as the Lord's slave (Isaiah 42:1–4; 49:1–6; 50:4–11; 52:13–53:12).

266. KJV Matthew 12:18 translates *pais* as "servant" (compare with Isaiah 42:1–4).

267. Strong's G1247; see Blue Letter Bible, "Dictionary and Word Search for *diakoneō (Strong's 1247)*," 1996–2011, 5 March 2011, http://www.blueletterbible.org/lang/lexicon/lexicon.cfm?Strongs=G1247&t=KJV.

268. In this instance, *diakoneō* is used in the same way the slaves who, after laboring all day in the fields, are asked to minister to the master of the house and feed him before they are allowed to eat and drink themselves (compare with Luke 17:8).

269. Matthew 4:19; Mark 8:34; John 13:15; 21:22; Hebrews 5:8; 1 Peter 2:21.

270. John 13:4–17.

271. Ephesians 6:14; 1 Peter 1:13; Doctrine and Covenants 27:15–16; 75:22.

272. Alberto Angela, *A Day in the Life of Ancient Rome*, translated by Gregory Conti, (New York: Europa Editions, 2009), 45–53.

273. A. Edersheim, *Sketches of Jewish Social Life in the Days of Christ* (Peabody, MA: Hendrickson Publishers, Inc., 1994), 198–99.

274. Bradley, *Slavery and Society at Rome*, 87–89.

275. John's account of Peter being "naked" while he fished indicates he was only wearing his loincloth (compare with John 21:7).

276. A girdle around the loins was the standard-issue battle dress for Roman soldiers. It was made of heavy leather, covered with brass plates, was situated just below the breastplate, and worn over the tunic. It was a foundation for carrying a sword, dagger,

and attaching the apron that extended downward and protected the thighs. They would "gird their loins" as a final preparation for battle by pulling up their tunics and tucking its hem into the leather girdle around their waist. This kept their tunic out of the way and allowed for better mobility and effectiveness as they moved across the battlefield.

277. Luke 17:8.

278. Luke 12:35–38.

279. Harris, *Slave of Christ*, 52, note 11.

280. John 13:8.

281. Doctrine and Covenants 88:139–41.

282. Matthew 26:39; 26:42; Mark 14:36; Luke 22:42; John 5:30.

283. Matthew 26:14–15; 27:3–10.

284. Exodus 21:32.

285. Philippians 2:6–11.

286. Hengel, *Crucifixion in the Ancient World*, 62.

287. 1 Corinthians 1:23.

288. James E. Talmage, *Jesus the Christ*, Classics in Mormon Literature edition (Salt Lake City: Deseret Book, 1982), 20–21.

289. 1 Corinthians 5:7.

290. Strong's G3083.

291. Blue Letter Bible, "Dictionary and Word Search for *lytron (Strong's 3083)*," 1996–2011, 1 March 2011, http://www.blueletterbible.org/lang/lexicon/lexicon.cfm?Strongs=G3083&t=KJV.

292. Strong's G3084.

293. 1 Peter 1:18–19.

294. Blue Letter Bible, "Dictionary and Word Search for *lytrōsis (Strong's 3085)*," 1996–2011, 6 March 2011, http://www.blueletterbible.org/lang/lexicon/lexicon.cfm?Strongs=G3085&t=KJV.

295. Hebrews 9:12.

296. Strong's G487.

297. Blue Letter Bible, "Dictionary and Word Search for anti-*lytron (Strong's 487)*," 1996–2011, 2 March 2011, http://www.blueletterbible.org/lang/lexicon/lexicon.cfm?Strongs=G487&t=KJV.

298. Ephesians 1:4.

299. Ephesians 1:5.

300. Ephesians 1:7.

301. Blue Letter Bible, "Dictionary and Word Search for *peripoiēsis (Strong's 4047)*," 1996–2011, 26 July 2011, http://www.blueletterbible.org/lang/lexicon/lexicon.cfm?Strongs=G4047&t=KJV.

302. 2 Thessalonians 2:13–14.

303. Hebrews 10:35–39.

304. Blue Letter Bible, "Dictionary and Word Search for *eklektos (Strong's 1588)*," 1996–2011, 27 July 2011, http://www.blueletterbible.org/lang/lexicon/lexicon.cfm?Strongs=G1588&t=KJV.

305. Blue Letter Bible, "Dictionary and Word Search for *periousios (Strong's 4041)*," 1996–2011, 31 July 2011, http://www.blueletterbible.org/lang/lexicon/lexicon.cfm?Strongs=G4041&t=KJV.

306. See Thayer's lexicon for a definition of *bought* that's based on the original Greek word *agorazō*, which means "to do business, buy, or sell in the market place." In this context, we can state that this was a slave market. See Blue Letter Bible, "Dictionary and Word Search for *agorazō (Strong's 59)*," 1996–2011, 2 March 2011, http://www.blueletterbible.org/lang/lexicon/lexicon.cfm?Strongs=G59&t=KJV.

307. Acts 20:28.

308. 1 Corinthians 6:19–20.

309. See earlier chapter on Paul's imprisonment and tribulations.

310. That is to say, enslavement of sin; slaves of Christ; or prisoner of Christ.

311. Harris, *Slave of Christ*, 76.

312. Romans 8:21; 1 Corinthians 10:29; 2 Corinthians 3:17; Galatians 2:4; 5:1–13.

313. 1 Corinthians 7:22.

314. Romans 6:20; 7:3; 1 Corinthians 7:21–22, 39; 9:1, 19; 12:13; Galatians 3:28; 4:22–23, 26, 30–31; Ephesians 6:8; Colossians 3:11.

315. Romans 6:18, 22; 8:2, 21; Galatians 5:1.

316. L. Morris, *Galatians* (Downers Grove, IL: Intervarsity Press, 1996), as cited by Harris, *Slave of Christ*, 76–79.

317. Galatians 4:22–31.

318. Children of a bondwoman were not given the same birthright because a mother's slave status was passed on to her offspring. Legally speaking, Ishmael was not Abraham's son but his slave. The master had the option of adopting the children he fathered through his slaves, and often did. Paul's teaching on adoption in Galatians 4:1–7 takes the already immense blessings of our ransom from enslavement of sin to even greater levels.

319. Galatians 4:31.

320. Galatians 4:7.

321. Galatians 2:4.

322. Harris, *Slave of Christ*, 153–54.

323. *Ibid.*, 154.

324. Card, *A Better Freedom*, 24.

325. *Ibid.*, 86 and footnote 30, citing Euripedes, *Helena*, 728–31; *Ion*, 854–56; Seneca, *De Beneficiis*, 3.20.1; *Epistulae*, 47.17.

326. John MacArthur, *Slave* (Nashville, TN: Thomas Nelson, 2010), 197.

327. 2 Nephi 2:5, 18, 27; Alma 12:26; 42:11; Mormon 9:4.

328. 2 Nephi 2:18.

329. 2 Nephi 2:27.

330. Moses 1:22.

331. 2 Peter 2:12–19.

332. Acts 8:23.

333. John 10:10–15 (compare with Alma 5:39–41).

334. Philippians 4:6.

335. Romans 8:28.

336. Hebrews 8:12; 10:17; Colossians 2:13–14; Doctrine and Covenants 58:42.

337. Hebrews 13:5–6; Psalm 23; Doctrine and Covenants 84:88.

338. Romans 8:35–39.

339. Philippians 4:7; see also MacArthur, *Slave*, 94–95.

340. Romans 6:18–23.

341. Matthew 11:28–30; Romans 14:18; 2 Corinthians 5:9; Hebrews 13:21; 1 Thessalonians 4:1.

342. MacArthur, *Slave*, 76–77.

343. See John 6:66.

344. Gamaliel the Elder (Rabban Gamaliel), mentor of the Apostle Paul (Acts 22:3) and prominent Pharisee, was an influential doctor of Jewish law. He played a large role in the Sanhedrin during the first century and was highly esteemed of the people (Acts 5:34–40). In the *Ethics of the Fathers*, Gamaliel is quoted as saying, "Make for yourself a teacher, and remove yourself from doubt, and do not make a habit of tithing by estimate" (Mishna, *Pirkei Avot*, 1:16).

345. John 1:35–51.

346. MacArthur, *Slave*, 16–17.

347. Matthew 25:14–30; compare to Luke 19:12–27 for the parable of the pounds or minas.

348. Luke 19:12.

349. John 15:16.

350. "Yea doubtless, and I count all things but loss for the excellency of the knowledge of Christ Jesus my Lord: for whom I have suffered the loss of all things, and do count them but dung, that I may win Christ, and be found in him, not having mine own righteousness, which is of the law, but that which is through the faith of Christ, the righteousness which is of God by faith: that I may know him, and the power of his resurrection, and the fellowship of his sufferings, being made conformable unto his death; if by any means I might attain unto the resurrection of the dead. Not as though I had already attained, either were already perfect: but I follow after, if that I may apprehend that for which also I am apprehended of Christ Jesus" (Philippians 3:8–12).

351. Romans 1:7; 1 Corinthians 1:2; Ephesians 1:18.

352. MacArthur, *Slave*, 10–14 and footnote 9.

353. 1 Corinthians 1:11, 16.

354. 1 Corinthians 15:23; Galatians 5:24.

355. Martin, *Slavery as Salvation,* 30.

356. Philippians 2:5–11.

357. Philo, *De Cherubim*, 107, as quoted by Harris, *Slave of Christ*, 136.

358. Acts 11:26; compare with Acts 26:28; 1 Peter 4:16.

359. Ignatius, *Epistle to the Romans*, 1:10–11.

360. MacArthur, *Slave*, 7–15.

361. Eusebius, *Church History*, 5.1.20–24, 37–39, as is quoted in MacArthur, *Slave*, 7–8.

362. James Spencer Northcote, *Epitaphs of the Catacombs or Christian Inscriptions in Rome During the First Four Centuries* (London: Longman, Green & Co., 1878), 139–40, as quoted in MacArthur, *Slave*, 8–9.

363. MacArthur, *Slave*, 45.

364. Matthew 28:19; Acts 8:16; 10:48; 19:5. Compare with Acts 2:38; 22:16; Romans 6:3; 1 Corinthians 1:13; Galatians 3:27.

365. Harris, *Slave of Christ*, 109–10.

366. Such references are not limited to the New Testament. See also 2 Nephi 31:13; Mosiah 5:7–9; Helaman 3:28; 3 Nephi 27:5–6; Doctrine and Covenants 18:21–24.

367. Acts 2:21, 36–38.

368. 2 Samuel 22:4; Psalm 18:3; Jeremiah 23:6; 33:16. See also Alma 9:17 and Doctrine and Covenants 100:17.

369. Acts 3.

370. Acts 3:4.

371. Isaiah 61:1–3.

372. Luke 4:22.

373. Luke 4:28–29.

374. Mark 6:5.

375. Harris, *Slave of Christ*, 76.

376. Angela, *A Day in the Life of Ancient Rome*, 65–67.

377. Martin, *Slavery as Salvation,* 64.

378. Blue Letter Bible, "Dictionary and Word Search for *apeleutheros (Strong's 558),*" 1996–2011, 2 April 2011, http://www.blueletterbible.org/lang/lexicon/lexicon.cfm?Strongs=G558&t=KJV.

379. Blue Letter Bible, "Dictionary and Word Search for *eleutheros (Strong's 1658),*" 1996–2011, 2 April 2011, http://www.blueletterbible.org/lang/lexicon/lexicon.cfm?strongs=G1658&t=KJV.

380. "Somewhere I read a statement that the function of a newspaper is to comfort the afflicted and to afflict the comforted. In some respects, I think, this is what the Church is all about—to comfort the afflicted and to afflict the comforted. We are to care for the needy, the fatherless, the widows. In the words of the Savior, we are to care for those who are 'an hungred,' 'thirsty,' 'a stranger,' 'naked,' 'sick,' and 'in prison.' (Harold B. Lee, *New Era*, January 1971, 4. See the original quote in 1902 "Newspaper Publicity" in *Observations of Mr. Dooley* by Peter Finley Dunne).

381. Ephesians 4:13.

382. Genesis 12; Abraham 2.

383. Exodus 2:1–10.

384. *The Institutes*, book 1, Internet Medieval Source Book, 2 April 2011, http://www.fordham.edu/halsall/basis/535institutes.html; source: Oliver J. Thatcher, editor, the Library of Original Sources (Milwaukee: University Research Extension Company, 1907),

vol. III: The Roman World, 100–66. Scanned in and modernized by Dr. Jerome S. Arkenberg, Department of History, California State Fullerton.

385. Veyne, *A History of Private Life*, 17–18.

386. Robert Paulissian, "Adoption in Ancient Assyria and Babylonia," *Journal of Ancient Assyrian Academic Studies*, 13 (2), 1999, 5–34. See also Roland De Vaux, *Ancient Israel: It's Life and Institutions* (Grand Rapids, MI: Wm. B. Eerdmans Publishing Company, 1997), 51–52.

387. Cicero, *Philippics*, 13.11.24–25.

388. Matthew 3:9; John 8:37.

389. Acts 7:20–23.

390. Galatians 3:13.

391. Galatians 3:26–29. Compare with Doctrine and Covenants 84:33–39.

392. Galatians 4:1–3.

393. Galatians 5:1.

394. Romans 8:2.

395. Romans 8:15.

396. Romans 8:21.

397. Ephesians 4:6–8; Doctrine and Covenants 14:7.

398. Revelation 21:3–7.

399. Moses 6:67–68.

400. Doctrine and Covenants 34:3; 45:8.

401. Doctrine and Covenants 84:38.

402. Exodus 21:2; Deuteronomy 15:12.

403. Exodus 21:5–6; Deuteronomy 15:16–17.

404. John Gill, "Commentary on Exodus 21:6," *The New John Gill Exposition of the Entire Bible*, 10 April 2011, http://www.searchgodsword.org/com/geb/view.cgi?book=ex&chapter=021&verse=006.

405. Adam Clarke, "Commentary on Exodus 21," *The Adam Clarke Commentary*, 10 April 2011, http://www.studylight.org/com/acc/view.cgi?book=ex&chapter=021.

406. Galatians 6:17.

407. John 15:16.

408. Matthew 10:38; 16:24; Mark 8:34; 10:21; Luke 9:23; 14:27.

409. Newport J. D. White, *A Translation of the Latin Writings of St. Patrick* (London: The Society for Promoting Christian Knowledge, 1918).

410. Patrick's writings from the early fifth century are some of the only writings that give us the perspective of a great Christian who was once a slave. Though many slaves later went on to write, none have written about their experiences with quite his perspective.

411. *Confession*, verse 1.

412. *Ibid.*, verse 16.

413. *Ibid.*, verse 42.

414. *Ibid.*, verse 23.

415. *Ibid.*, verse 61.

416. *Ibid.*

417. *Ibid.*, verse 28.

418. *Ibid.*, verses 37, 52, 55.

419. *Ibid.*, verse 41.

420. *Ibid.*, verse 50.

421. *Epistle*, verse 3.

422. *Ibid.*, verse 4.

423. Patrick's letter actually excommunicated Coroticus and his men.

424. In keeping with the pattern seen throughout the New Testament, Patrick's original Latin word for slave (*servos*) is translated as "servant." See Newport J. D. White, *Libri Sancti Patricii—The Latin Writings of St. Patrick* (Dublin: The University Press, 1905) 193.

425. *Epistle*, verse 7.

426. *Ibid.*, verse 10.

427. *Confession*, verse 15.

428. See also Mosiah 5:5–7 for a second Book of Mormon example of this doctrine.

429. Matthew 25:14–30.

430. Luke 19:11–27.

431. Galatians 1:10.

432. *Oiketēs:* a household slave or domestic. See Blue Letter Bible, "Dictionary and Word Search for *oiketēs (Strong's 3610)*," 1996–2011, 13 April 2011, http://www.blueletterbible.org/lang/lexicon/lexicon.cfm?Strongs=G3610&t=KJV.

433. Blue Letter Bible, "Dictionary and Word Search for *kaleō (Strong's 2564)*," 1996–2011, 13 April 2011, http://www.blueletterbible.org/lang/lexicon/lexicon.cfm?strongs=G2564&t=KJV&page=5.

434. 1 Peter 2:16. The word that is translated as *using (echō)* means "to have, to hold, to own or possess." See also Blue Letter Bible,

"Dictionary and Word Search for *echō (Strong's 2192)*," 1996–2011, 13 April 2011, http://www.blueletterbible.org/lang/lexicon/lexicon.cfm?Strongs=G2192&t=KJV.

435. 1 Thessalonians 1:9.

436. Blue Letter Bible, "Dictionary and Word Search for *douloō (Strong's 1402)*," 1996–2011, 10 April 2011, http://www.blueletterbible.org/lang/lexicon/lexicon.cfm?Strongs=G1402&t=KJV.

437. Romans 6:12–18.

438. Romans 6:17.

439. Romans 7:25.

440. Blue Letter Bible, 1996–2011, 13 April 2011, http://www.blueletterbible.org/lang/lexicon/lexicon.cfm?Strongs=G1396&t=KJV.

441. 2 Corinthians 10:4–5.

442. Romans 7:23.

443. Romans 12:1.

444. See also John 15:5–8.

445. Neal A. Maxwell said, "So many of us are kept from eventual consecration because we mistakenly think that, somehow, by letting our will be swallowed up in the will of God, we lose our individuality (see Mosiah 15:7). What we are really worried about, of course, is not giving up self, but selfish things—like our roles, our time, our preeminence, and our possessions. No wonder we are instructed by the Savior to lose ourselves (see Luke 9:24). He is only asking us to lose the old self in order to find the new self. It is not a question of one's losing identity but of finding his true identity! Ironically, so many people already lose themselves anyway in their consuming hobbies and preoccupations but with far, far lesser things." He went on to say that "the submission of one's will is really the only

uniquely personal thing we have to place on God's altar" (Neal A. Maxwell, "Swallowed Up in the Will of the Father," *Ensign*, November 1995).

446. Luke 12:32.

447. Matthew 7:21; 12:50.

448. John 5:36–37; 6:38–44; 8:16–18; 12:49; 13:3; 16:28; 17:25; 20:21.

449. John 5:19, 30, 43; 6:38–39; 8:28–29; 14:31; 15:9–10; 15:15; 18:11.

450. John 18:10–11. It is noteworthy that all four Gospels preserve the account of the slave of the high priest being assaulted by Peter at the arrest of Jesus (compare with Matthew 26:51–53; Mark 14:47; Luke 22:49–51). Only Luke, the physician, records that, as one of His final miracles, Jesus restored the severed ear of Malchus. As a fellow healer of men, it was a detail that would have been forever etched in his mind. And this incident is the ultimate proof that those who seek a sign will never be satisfied when the sign is produced. It is interesting that Jesus was never charged with the assault on Malchus, even though a reasonable case could be made that He was an accessory. In light of the Sanhedrin's desperate search for charges to bring against Jesus, this is a significant detail. It firstly suggests that Malchus was indeed healed by Jesus. Secondly, it reiterates the social reality that assaulting a slave—even to the point of striking his head with a sword—was somehow not that all big of a deal. A man could certainly be liable for damaging another's slave. But no court of the day would argue that violence against a slave was worthy of the death penalty. He was just a slave. It is yet another example of how pitiable the existence of a slave was.

451. Andrew C. Skinner, *Gethsemane* (Salt Lake City: Deseret Book, 2002), 6.

452. For parallel accounts of this incident, see Matthew 26:39–42 and Mark 14:35–36.

453. *History of the Church*, vol. 2, 176.

454. Joseph Smith, *Lectures on Faith*, compiled by N. B. Lundwell (Salt Lake City: Deseret Book, 1985) 6:7.

455. Doctrine and Covenants 1:38; 68:3–4.

456. Luke 15:11–32.

457. Romans 6:11.

Scripture Index

Genesis

Exodus

Leviticus

Numbers

Deuteronomy

Joshua

Judges

Ruth

1 Samuel

2 Samuel

1 Kings

Psalms

Isaiah

Mark

Luke

Acts

Romans

1 Corinthians

2 Corinthians

Galatians

Ephesians

Philippians

Colossians

1 Thessalonians

2 Thessalonians

1 Timothy

2 Timothy

Titus

Philemon

Hebrews

James

1 Peter

2 Peter

1 John

Jude

Revelation

2 Nephi

Mosiah

Alma

Helaman

3 Nephi

Mormon

Doctrine and Covenants

Moses

Abraham

Joseph Smith—History

Articles of Faith

ABOUT THE AUTHOR

W. REID LITCHFIELD is an endocrinologist from Henderson, Nevada. He is a graduate of Brigham Young University (BS) and University of Calgary (MD) and completed his endocrinology fellowship at Harvard Medical School. In addition to a number of scientific publications, he has published medical history papers entitled "On the Physical Death of Jesus Christ" and "The Bittersweet Demise of Herod the Great." He is the recipient of several Top Doctor Awards, as well as professional awards for leadership in his community and medical society. You can find more of his writings on his blog at www.reidlitchfield.com.